MW00682635

expect success
BE UnStoppable

a woman's secret recipe

julie henderson

GLASTONBURY PRESS · SAN RAFAEL, CALIFORNIA

ISBN 978-0-944963-13-5
Printed in USA
Book design by Sara Patton

For any inquiries or questions about quantity discounts or permission to
use quotes, please contact:
Glastonbury Press LLC
454 Las Gallinas #108
San Rafael, CA 94903
info@glastonburypress.com

To my husband Bill, with love and affection, for his kind spirit, quiet strength and caring heart.

To my sons, Jeff and Pat, who inspire me with their vibrancy and energy.

You are all a blessing.

CONTENTS

ACKNOWLEDGMENTS

A lot of wonderful people helped to complete this book. Misty Forsman, publisher, coach, editor, and friend, gave unwavering enthusiasm and constant encouragement. Without her this book would not have become a reality. Also, special thanks to Peggy Murrah, Darrell Wingerak, Kenn White, Andy Wibbels, Dan Kern, Kathi and Hobie Dunn, Sara Patton, and Areanne Lloyd.

Also, Mary-Lynne Kenneth-Kwon, Cathy Perkins, Anny Tielman, Emma Osman, Bernice Craig, and Sheila, Darlene, Benita, Marge, Debbie, Jennifer, Lynn, Vanessa, Julie, Heather, Robin, Monica, and Pam, you are all most appreciated.

Special acknowledgement to my sister Pat—my constant companion working together on the farm with Dad. She has also been my dearest friend throughout the years,

My family has been part of this book throughout. My dad who is in heaven, where I hope he is watching the completion of this book, I thank you for the lessons and the memories. And Mom, thank you for your tireless dedication to our family. My brother and sisters who were part of all the fun times growing up on the farm, thank you.

A NOTE TO YOU FROM JULIE ...

I am just a very simple person who learned to be determined, strong-willed and persistent. This, I learned, is important and needed to achieve your dreams.

I knew I had to hold onto my dreams. I also learned that I cannot do it all by myself. Yet, I needed to make the main efforts myself if it was going to be.

All of us have a life story filled with trials and tribulations, and as my coach told me, we can help people by sharing our story ... so we can inspire others to do the same. That was what moved me to write this book.

On a final note, I want to emphasize that everything in life is a choice. We create our reality. Choosing to accept where you are, or perhaps conforming in order to avoid confrontation, are choices. At the end of the day, we need to realize that we came into this world alone and we go out alone. Ask yourself, "Am I existing or am I am really living?" What is it that you were meant to do? Whatever your dream, know that your dream loves you and you have to believe you have that dream for a reason.

Find your passion and go for it!

Julie Henderson
Manitoba, Canada

1

Lesson in a Wheelchair

*Be bold and courageous. When you look back
on your life you'll regret the things you didn't
do far more than the ones you did.*

– H. Jackson Brown, Jr.

Oftentimes, when something life-changing occurs, we make decisions about our lives. These are the "wake-up" calls that can send us either into a depression, thinking that we can't do anything to help ourselves, or into a new state of awareness of how we can react positively to adverse situations in our lives.

Many of us have had to suffer through accidents—in a car or on a bike or in a boat. Whatever the vehicle, experiencing the discombobulating feeling of an accident can jolt you out of your complacency. It can make you take notice of where you are in that moment. Sometimes, it can be life-changing. Mine was. I made a decision because of what happened to me, one that has shaded many of my other decisions that I've made in life. Here's what happened.

Easily, I can recall the events; I was 23 years old and married. My husband was a full-time student at a technical school some distance away in another province.

I had been visiting my sister, Pat, over the weekend. Our time together was mostly doing simple things and enjoying each other's company.

On Sunday, she sang in church, while I played the piano. I wasn't very good at the piano, but she was a beautiful singer, and I teased her to sing loud to drown out the piano!

After church we had lunch, then I left for home as I was playing baseball that night in an amateur ladies league.

There were two different roads to my home town. On the "long" way, the road was paved. On my return trip, I decided to take the "short" way, about an hour less, but most of it was a narrow gravel road.

It was a blistering hot, clear day, and you could not see behind the car because it was incredibly dusty. The dust just hung in the air because there was no wind.

I drove for 40 minutes. Then I noticed a vehicle approaching. I had a creepy feeling and thought to myself, "I have to pull over to the right." Any car behind that car would not be able to see me before the dust cleared. I slowed right down, and I remember steering my car so that it was halfway in the ditch.

That was that last thing I remember before coming to and seeing the blood on the steering wheel and feeling it drip from my face.

When I next looked up, I saw two guys at my car. I asked the two guys what happened.

They told me they were tired of eating the dust from the vehicle in front of them and decided to pass it. I remember thinking, "Tired! You didn't even think if you could see ahead or not?"

It was a head-on car collision. I remember thanking God that I was alive.

The two guys that collided with me helped me to maneuver my feet around the brake pedal and get me out of the car and into the ditch. I didn't want to be near the car, in case it blew up!

Then they told me they had to get to work for their shift, so they jumped a ride with someone else that came by and took off!

I was still lying in the ditch when some other people came by. One young woman stayed by my side until the ambulance arrived many, many hours later. Her name was Lorraine Harris, and she brought me a sleeping bag to lie on and reassured me I was fine. I asked her how I looked, worrying I had lost some teeth. She comforted me saying the same thing happened to her in a car accident. I still don't know to this day if that was true. But that does not matter. She was a godsend, and I will be eternally grateful to her for being my angel.

It was a dreadful wait, lying in the ditch among the dry grass, weeds and rocks. My accident couldn't have happened in a more remote location in a densely forested area where bears, coyote, fox and other creatures lived. I prayed that help would come quickly … I needed to stay strong. I knew that I had several injuries and I knew it was important that I get medical attention immediately. I wasn't sure if I had any internal injuries. My legs throbbed with a dull, constant pain, and my face and mouth ached as I lay praying for help. Fear and shock kept me shaking.

The sound of the sirens of the ambulance arriving was the sweetest music. I had waited, lying in the ditch, for over three hours. Help had finally arrived!

Lorraine had done a wonderful job keeping me comfortable. The attendants bandaged my legs and wrapped me in warm blankets.

I felt then and there that I was going to be okay. I knew I had *survived* my car accident.

The ambulance arrived at the hospital at 10:30 PM.

Seconds later I was taken into emergency. The doctors examined me quickly and then told me that they couldn't put my bones together as well as a specialist. They told me that they were making arrangements to fly me immediately by air ambulance to a city four hours away.

I was rushed to the air ambulance. The ride seemed quick and the morphine was a welcome relief, and the pain subsided.

Five hours later, I awoke from the operation and learned about my extensive injuries.

I had several pins in both of my broken ankles and casings shoved up my broken nose. I also broke my cheekbone and lost five teeth. Two days later they pulled the roots of the broken teeth.

My mouth was sore!

No one called or came to see me for two days.

Finally, after being alone all that time, my husband and family came to visit at the hospital in the intensive care unit, where I remained for a week.

On the first day I was allowed to leave my room, I wanted to go to the lounge so I wheeled myself in my wheelchair. I pushed the double doors open with my wheelchair and there in front of me were these two really old guys!

I must have looked like I had been in some huge battle with my casts on and no teeth, and I was black and blue from head to foot.

They both looked at me and laughed!

Now these guys didn't look a whole lot different from me, except they were old; they were both in wheelchairs and they both had toothless grins too!

One guy laughed and said, "What did the *other* guy look like?"

At first, I was a little offended. I could very easily have gotten really angry with them because they were insensitive and uncaring about my injuries.

But instead of reacting badly, *I chose to laugh.* I laughed with them because I could see myself in their eyes, and I really did look funny.

And laughing instead of crying or getting angry defined this whole experience for me. It prompted me to make a major life decision. I realized *I (always) have a choice to be positive AND not feel sorry for myself.* As Lloyd Alexander said:

> *Optimism is essential to achievement and it is also the foundation of courage and true progress.*

Ever since that moment, I have actively chosen the positive, no matter what the situation, and it has been an invaluable attitude to take. And believe me, I had to practice it every day.

I was so happy to finally have the pins out of my feet and I drove home. It was the first time since the car accident that I was able to drive and there was no way I even contemplated not driving. At 23, I was far too independent to let one accident scare me from driving again. I was back at work the following Monday, and I was a happy girl!

And I have, by and large, stayed a happy girl. Since then, my initial "stay positive" mantra has expanded to include the idea that it's not what happens that determines our life's future: it is what we do about what happens. What happens ... happens!

Jim Rohn, motivational speaker, uses the image of a sailboat in which he points out that it is the not the blowing of the wind that determines our destination; it is the set of the sail. The same wind blows on us all: the wind of disaster, the wind of opportunity, the wind of change, the favorable wind and the unfavorable wind. The economic wind, the social wind and the political wind—the same wind blows on everybody.

The difference in where you arrive in one year, three years or five is not the blowing of the wind, it is *the set of the sail*.

He goes on to say that if we wish to change, we can. It doesn't matter what age you are, just decide to change and do it … if you *want* to!

For things to change, *you* have to change for the better. Don't wish things were easier. Wish you were better. Don't wish for fewer problems. Wish for more skills. Don't wish for less challenge. Wish for more wisdom. Accept the challenge, because you cannot grow without a challenge. Develop the wisdom to overcome the challenge. And finally, you can do the most remarkable things, no matter what happens. Humans can do the most remarkable things.

This is the philosophy that we all can adopt in order to change our life.

"A bend in the road is not the end of the road," Joan Lunden said. My accident helped me to see the deep wisdom in that. I had challenges, but I took hold of my mind and focused on seeing the good and maintained a positive outlook. If I had not, I would have been doomed.

Like many of you reading this book, I have experienced much hardship and heartache in my life.

I kept on "keeping on" and was able to create a very good life for myself. And my lesson in the wheelchair has always helped me to get through the difficult times. Even though it is sometimes very difficult to do, and sometimes I forget for a few moments (or hours, even) to look for the positive, I eventually do so, and that has helped keep me strong.

And that is my wish for you: to find your strength as a person and as a wonderful and creative person who has much to offer this world.

Live with the attitude of gratitude—you have so much to be thankful for. Be thankful for what you have. If there is something you want to change—do it. Life is fragile, and you don't have to have a car accident to have a wake-up call. Go and live with purpose.

Notes

✦ We all have had challenges throughout our life. If your life was nearing its end, list some regrets you would have.

> Regrets about yourself?
> About your family?
> Your friends?
> Your accomplishments?

✦ What "unfinished" wishes, dreams and hopes would you have that would bother you? List some wishes you had for yourself that you never fulfilled.

✦ Is there anything special you "were going to do" but never did?

✦ Is there any place you wish you could have visited?

✦ Any other serious regrets?

✦ Is there something special you would like to do before you die?

Good news!
You still have time!

✦ Write down a date when you will begin.

Dream Big

If your dream doesn't require a miracle,
then it isn't big enough.

– John Di Lemme

Martin Luther King Jr. said: "Now, I say to you today my friends, even though we face the difficulties of today and tomorrow, I still have a dream. It is a dream deeply rooted in the American dream. I have a dream that one day this nation will rise up and live out the true meaning of its creed: "We hold these truths to be self-evident, that all men are created equal."

I felt I've had a pretty good life and I have always been grateful for what I have, so I felt I shouldn't want for more when others had less. Yet, I couldn't deny the fact that at one point I wanted a bigger house with a two-car garage, and I wanted to travel and have other nice things like other people. Twenty years ago I often dreamed of what it would be like to not ever have to sweep the snow off the car in the winter before leaving for work, not to mention the comfort of a warm vehicle.

Martin Luther King's "I Have a Dream" speech shows how strong a force language can be to communicate new ways of thinking. King was able to spread his ideas and bring about many positive changes in his country, the "United States of America." Martin Luther King knew how to effectively use the power of words to effect change in his society.

I am continually reminded that each of us has the capacity to create a better vision of life, for ourselves and the world around us, if only we will make the effort to do so. It is my desire to find the courage to create a future vision, and bring that vision into being. My cup will overflow, and it will allow me to fill other people's cups.

When I remarried, my husband and I wanted to purchase a new home, but none were available. Often in the evenings, I would ride my bike in the newest area in the community—it was a beautiful location. I absolutely loved one house in particular. It was situated in the middle of the bay and there were 12 homes in that location. It was a beautiful house and it had a huge pie-shaped lot, underground sprinklers, manicured lawn with shrubs and trees, a huge deck, a two-car garage and a large garage at the back for storage. Behind the house was a pond. It was a great location. As I rode my bike, I admired the home and the location. I would think: "I would just love to live in that house, but the house will never come up for sale. Who would ever move from there?"

Three months later, I got a call from our Realtor and friend, Ed. He was calling to tell me that the house I had been admiring for months was for sale and asked if we were still interested in it. Well! I could hardly contain myself at work! I quickly phoned my husband and told him the news. I was emphatic. I said, "I have to have that house!" We quickly started making plans to sell our house so we could purchase the new home.

Did you know it is our birthright to be prosperous and have abundance? Mark Gorman, author of *God's Plan for Prosperity*, said: "If God didn't want us to be rich, why did he create Heaven?" Randy Gage in his Prosperity Series says it is a sin to be poor. He goes on to say if we are not prosperous, we're missing the mark that the Creator intended for us. We were born rich and prosperous. Our Father wants us to be prosperous and have the entire Kingdom! So dream *big*!

We listed our house in September and we had some interest, but no buyer. It was a stressful process, and keeping up with the house with two small children, while working full-time, was exhausting. By the time Christmas came, I pretty much gave up hope, because I thought, "Who is going to buy a house at Christmas time?" People are busy with Christmas and the expense. It would take a miracle for it to happen! I just decided to relax and accept that we would not be moving any time soon and decided that if it was going to be, it would be. Then on January 7, I got a call from Ed saying that one of the couples who had looked at our house a few months before decided they wanted to purchase it. My goodness! I felt like I had won the lottery! We quickly put in an offer for the new home and three weeks later we were in the house. It was amazing!

This goes to show that when you dream *big* and "place your order" to the universe, it will manifest.

> *Get excited and enthusiastic about your own*
> *dream. This excitement is like a forest fire—you*
> *can smell it, taste it and see it from a mile away.*

– Denis Waitley

Since that time, at the beginning of the year, every morning I write out the miracles I want to manifest, and it has been amazing. The most important thing I learned through this exercise is that I have to be more and do more in order to have more. You can do this too. Figure out what you want, write it down and take action toward your goal. If you do that on a consistent basis you will have a life of prosperity and abundance. I guarantee it!

If you want to be larger than life, you need a dream that's larger than life. Small dreams won't serve you or anyone else. It takes the same amount of time to dream small as it does to dream big. So be *big* and be *bold*!

Dream Big — Notes

Here is how you can start to manifest your dream. Stop right now and do this!

Write down your *one* biggest dream: one dream that excites you the most. Remember, don't be small and realistic; be bold and unrealistic!

After you've written down your dream, list every single reason why you *can* achieve your dream. Don't even think about why you can't achieve your dream. Here are the steps:

+ Write down, or record, your *one* biggest dream: the one dream that excites you the most. If you record it, transcribe it to a page or pages you can read.

+ Make it *very detailed*. Write out or record every detail as you imagine living that dream.

+ Read it at least twice a day, morning and evening. Read it out loud at least once a day.

✦ After a week, re-write and/or record it as a *bigger* dream. Then read it at least twice a day—read it out loud at least once a day also.

✦ Did you *dream big*? Most of us have to re-do our *big* dream as we tend to shy away from our really big dreams. I encourage you to really *dream big* for yourself!

STEP OUT IN FAITH

If your life is going along famously and you are happy in your relationship and happy with your job, then consider yourself a very blessed woman or man!

But, *if you are tolerating people or things that no longer work for you and you feel like you can't spend another day living like you are, then why are you*? Think about that!? If the idea of making a change scares you, it is understandable, but if you just step out in faith, you will be amazed by your strength of character. This characteristic will empower you to create the life you want.

Some years ago, a friend gave me a card and on the front was a quote by Eleanor Roosevelt: "Do one thing every day that scares you." At the time I was in a job where I would come back home every day feeling drained, and I was very unhappy. My job title was Manager, Student Services, and my job was to sell training programs to people who were looking to upgrade their skills. Many of the potential clients were people whose jobs had been eliminated and were now unemployed and qualified for unemployment insurance. When people came to me to learn about what programs we had to offer, I also made it a point to take the time to ensure the training was in line with their goals. It was devastating for people to lose their jobs, and I found some job satisfaction because I was able to spend time listening to them and encouraging them by giving them hope for their future and potential employment opportunities. Some of the people had been in their jobs for 20 or 30 years with the same company. It gave me a lot of satisfaction when they thanked me for listening and for my encouragement and support.

I decided to step out in faith and quit my job! I had never quit a job in my life!

The thing about me quitting was I had no other job to go to. I applied for many, but I didn't have any interviews lined up. I have to admit, I was scared about not having a job to go to. Truthfully, I felt a bit sick quitting, but I decided I had to step out in faith and trust that I would find other work. And I did, but it took almost a year! That was a most difficult and frustrating time because I felt that my future was at the mercy of some employer. It is my belief that all situations we experience are meant to serve a purpose as a way for us to learn to trust and to have faith.

Brian Tracy, one of the world's leading authorities on personal and business success, has done extensive research on belief, and he states that the level of our success has an exact relationship to our faith, or belief in our success. He goes so far to say about our doubts that to the exact degree that we doubt our success, that is the exact degree that our success will be.

Your doubt is the limiting variable.

Your goals, minus your doubts, equal your reality.

– Ralph S. Marston, Jr.

ARE YOU SO SCARED TO FAIL THAT YOU DON'T EVEN TRY?

The testing of your faith is an outstanding way to create belief in yourself as part of your personal growth journey. You can test your faith quite easily by simply setting an important goal and not quitting prior to having reached it.

Unfortunately, many people wait to have faith before they make the big leap, but it doesn't work that way. You step out in faith: you must leap before the net appears—and believe that the net will appear, that you will land on your feet! Les Brown said: "Jump and grow wings on the way down!" When you prove to yourself that you're committed to creating real change in your life, the faith will come! By taking one step at a time, you will begin to feel your confidence grow. Every action you take raises your self-esteem and your belief in yourself. I have found this to be true in my life.

*Take the first step in faith. You don't have to see
the whole staircase, just take the first step.*

– Dr. Martin Luther King Jr.

Our faith expands each time we take action. Les Brown says if you are not willing to take risks, you cannot grow; if you do not grow, you cannot be happy; if you are not happy, then what is there to live for?

If I never took a step in faith and quit my job as Manager, Student Services, I never would have had the opportunity to start my own nutrition consulting business. With each new opportunity, I had challenges, but I continued to step out in faith and it gave me confidence to explore new opportunities.

If you are still contemplating whether you should "go for it," I encourage you to step out in faith and follow your heart. Brian Tracy found that every single successful person he ever spoke to had a turning point and the turning point was the moment where they made a clear, specific, unequivocal decision that they were not going to live like this anymore. That they were going to achieve success. Some people make that decision at 15 and some people make it at 50 ... most people never make it at all.

Are You So Scared to Fail That You Don't Even Try? — Notes

+ What would you do—what would you try—if you knew you *could not* fail?

+ Is that thought scary?

+ What is the worst thing that could happen if what you did, or tried, didn't work or did not turn out great?

+ How would you feel if you were to just "go for it?"

NEVER GIVE UP

Accrding to Og Mandino: whenever you make a mistake or get knocked down by life, don't look back at it too long. Mistakes are life's way of teaching you. Your capacity for occasional blunders is inseparable from your capacity to reach your goals. No one wins them all, and your failures, when they happen, are just part of your growth. Shake off your blunders. How will you know your limits without an occasional failure? Never quit. Your turn will come.

People who see challenges and obstacles as temporary and as valuable learning experiences are the ones who never quit. If you learn from your experiences, not repeating what didn't work in the past, and if you choose to never quit, your success is inevitable.

British Prime Minister Winston Churchill said during World War II: "… never give up, never give up." Churchill had a goal that was really important to him—stopping Hitler. You might say it was a matter of life or death. But not every goal is that important, and no goal should be engraved in stone.

As you go through life's changes, your desires will change too. However that doesn't mean giving up. Going after goals, to make your life the best it can be, involves a process of discovery. And that's why you should never give up.

When I recognized there wasn't a demand for my nutritional consulting services and it didn't seem like that would change in the short term, I decided that there was no point investing more time and money in the business. I then got involved with another business, and after a couple years decided I wasn't seeing the results and made another change. This time, my decision to join a company was for the wrong reason, and I quickly realized that it wasn't going to work for me. I had a lot of starts and stops in finding the right business, and it was very frustrating to accept that. When I thought about going back to a regular job, that thought made me feel depressed. I felt like I was giving up on my dream. I couldn't walk away from my dream.

What is it about giving up that provides temporary relief from obstacles? Although we may not like them, obstacles have a very important role in helping us stay focused and committed to our goals. I believe that obstacles are meant to help us strengthen our resolve to win. There is a Chinese proverb: "Fall down seven times, and get up eight."

Many have the illusion that life is supposed to be easy. It's not. The difficult fact is that life is hard for everyone. The main ingredient to all successful people is they are unwilling to ever give in to the stress and pressures of life. When setbacks and disappointments occur (as they will from time to time) this is the time to strengthen your resolve to win. It is never alright to give up on your dreams and goals. How will you know what you can achieve if you give up before you win? Not long ago, I heard someone say: "Most people don't quit at the bottom of the mountain, they quit halfway up, and then they miss out on the view from the top!"

Billionaire philanthropist and Presidential candidate H. Ross Perot said, "Most people stop digging three feet from the gold mine." Isn't that profound!

What are the gold mines you are digging for? For some it may be to develop a strong family life, for others to start that business. Whatever your personal gold mine is, you must develop the drive to say, "Nothing will stand in my way." I know there is nothing we can do to permanently rid ourselves of obstacles. However, we can be so thick-skinned that we refuse to allow our obstacles to stop us. Have the attitude that you will not quit three feet from your gold mine. You must persist till the end. You are only one idea away from a breakthrough.

Success is available to everyone, including you. The only thing that can hinder your success ultimately is you. When bad things come to us, we must creatively find a way to overcome them. We can do it. Bishop T.D. Jakes said: "The fact that you have a dream is the evidence that you have what it takes to achieve it." Never allow anyone or anything to cause you to stop digging for your personal gold mine. Success in any area of your life is totally possible for you if you will never give up.

Remember the quote: "Winners never quit, and quitters never win." I remember thinking after I read that, "Is that all I have to do to be a winner? All I have to do is never quit?" It seemed like a pretty simple principle to follow. As a young child, I was always expected to finish what I started, whether it was the food I put on my plate or the chores or picking rocks and roots. Never once did I think to say to my dad, "I don't feel like picking anymore rocks or roots." It wasn't an option. We had to keep working until Dad decided it was time to go in for lunch or dinner or it was too dark! I've learned that if I keep working toward my dream, even though there may be some detours along the way, sooner or later I will achieve my goal, if I do not quit.

The important thing to remember is that your dreams and goals will come to pass if you do not give up along the way. If you stop pursuit, you lose. Yet, if you adopt the attitude that you will not be denied, you really won't be denied. I'm not an expert on this, but I believe obstacles show up to help us become more resilient. Where you greatly desire to go, you can't be a whiner or a wimp. Les Brown says it best: "You must trade in who you've been for who you must become." Think about it. Look into the future and be brutally honest with yourself. What type of person must you be in the future in order to truly *be* who you greatly desire to be?

You may also find it helpful to examine the qualities and characteristics of successful people that you do not currently possess. What do you particularly like about that person? Are they friendlier, healthier, more confident, a better leader? Thoroughly analyze the ultimate you and the current you. When placed side by side, what changes must you make to become the ultimate you? Completing this exercise is very eye-opening.

One important thing that you will discover is the confident, resilient attitude that you really won't be denied. Success requires a different mindset. A big part of that mindset is developing a "never give up" mentality. It is possible for you to complete each task you begin with that mentality. Giving up robs you of the joy that's sure to come as you check off tasks that you've completed en route to your goal.

When you get into a tight place and everything goes against you, never give up then, for that is just the time that the tide will turn.

– Harriet Beecher Stowe

Too many people focus on the process, rather than the results. For instance, have you ever planned to go to the gym for a workout, but when your alarm went off, you rolled over to shut the alarm off and decided you were too tired, and just went back to sleep? It happened to me, and after that I vowed I would never make the excuse of being too tired to work out. I felt so lousy all that day for missing my workout, not only physically, but mentally. I had promised myself that I would work out daily, and by missing that one day, I let myself down. I felt so lethargic all day, too, and that was because I didn't have the same invigorating energy and enthusiasm that I do after my workout. I no longer miss a workout, and if even for a second I think I'd rather not go, I focus on how I will feel if I don't go; I focus on the results and not on the process.

These are the words of Jack Canfield: "You deserve to have your life exactly the way you want it." I believe that quote with everything within me. Your challenge is to believe this quote and realize that it may take a year, or two, or three for your life to be exactly as planned. Promise yourself that you will not give up along the way. Have confidence that you will make it through to the end. Keep going. Keep going. Keep going.

Never give up . . .
Never give up . . . Never give up.

You can do it! You, too, can take charge of your life. *You can*! I believe in you!

Never Give Up — Notes

Here are some daily tips that will contribute to your success:

1. Read personal development books and articles.

2. Participate in personal development programs.

3. Take consistent action.

4. Visualize how you will feel when you reach your goal.

5. Surround yourself with people who will support you.

6. Focus on the good.

+ List at least ten people you can name who have been a success.

    + Do you personally know any of these people?

    + Circle the ones you personally know.

    + Do you have both men and women on your list?
      If not, add the missing gender.

+ Why did they succeed? Timing? Luck? Special preparation?
  Or something else?

+ What unique, special qualities did they possess?

+ Were their special qualities what caused, or fueled, their success?

+ Do you possess any of these qualities?

+ Did they have a mentor? A coach?

Never give up … Never give up!

It's one or the other: pain or pleasure

Your chances of success are directly proportional
to the degree of pleasure you desire from
what you do. If you are in a job you hate,
face the fact squarely and get out.

– Michael Korda

Pain and pleasure are our greatest motivators. It's interesting how we will do anything to avoid pain, and it could be because all our lives we have learned to associate pain and pleasure with certain experiences based on the feedback we receive. Think of this. As a woman, you may have had challenges with your weight, and if you are overweight you know exactly what you need to do to lose weight but you don't. Why? It is because at some level you link more pain to dieting and exercise than to eating unhealthy foods and lying around on the couch all day.

Most of us know exactly what we need to do to make the necessary changes in our lives, but we don't do it. Change is one of those things no one wants to talk about. If we want to lose weight, we must change our schedule to include a daily workout regimen.

We spend far too much time thinking about whether we should or should not make a change.

We analyze it far too much and this creates "analysis paralysis." When we overanalyze, when we think too much, we become immobilized and stuck: it's called procrastination. Procrastination can be defined as our associations of what we link pain to. The longer we procrastinate the longer we stand still, and the longer we stand still the longer we settle for a life of mediocrity.

In my first marriage, I easily got caught in this web of procrastination, even though I definitely knew that I had to make a change. I would get hung up thinking about what people would say, and then I would question whether I could manage on my own. All these thoughts were creating some pain. But then I would think, "What will happen if I don't take action to make a change?" And because the answer to that question promised more pain, I was propelled into making a change.

I honestly believed that my relationship would improve once we were married, and I also honestly believed that having a baby would change our relationship. I was deluding myself by thinking that a baby would substitute for what was missing in my relationship. I felt that I did my best to compromise and accommodate my husband's needs. In the end, I just couldn't keep fixing him. I couldn't be someone I wasn't. We wanted different things out of life. If I would have agreed to go camping in the boondocks (that means tenting in remote areas), to not play ball, or curl in a women's league, to stay home and not take courses, to not have friends or my family visit, and to not go to social events, then maybe I would still be with him. And I would be a zombie by now!

It didn't give me any pleasure knowing I would hurt my husband by telling him I was unhappy and I no longer wanted to be with him. It certainly tugged at my heart to think about my son not having his parents in the same home. Yet, I felt more pain thinking of how I would feel if I didn't make a change versus the pain of staying in my marriage. So in order to overcome procrastination, I needed to focus on the long-term pain of what would happen if I didn't take action.

You may be someone who wants to get out of a relationship or maybe you want to change careers or perhaps lose weight. Here is something to contemplate: What would your answer to this question be: "If the next five years of your life are like the last five, where will you be?" What a profound statement, don't you think? You may find yourself living in what Anthony Robbins calls no-man's land, a place where "you're not really happy, but you're not unhappy enough to do anything about it."

If you are reading this book, you are someone who wants something out of life and you are actively pursuing it. You may even be trying to develop goals. The best way to do this is to get angry and disappointed about the way things currently are in your life and decide to do whatever it takes to move away from that negative feeling. The two guiding forces in our lives are pain and pleasure. We must be able to make the pain of not changing more painful than making the changes.

Success is available to all. No one is exempt. It is true that we do not all have the same education, resources and connections. The only even playing field we all possess is time and the fact that we create our own reality. What we decide to do with that time will determine the results that appear in our lives, both positive and negative.

Yesterday is gone. We must release the past so we can make forward progress into the future. Today is all we have. What we do with our today will determine whether our next five years are like our last five. Deepak Chopra said: "The way you think, the way you behave, the way you eat, can influence your life by 30 to 50 years." Each day, we choose. We are in control. We must make firm decisions that will inspire us to action despite the necessary changes required.

So ask yourself, "Is there something in my life that I would like to change?" Then, decide you want to make the change, feel the pain of disappointment and failure if you don't make the change; decide what habits, relationships and time-wasters are preventing you from getting what you want, and then make a list of the positive habits, relationships and time management systems needed to create the success.

Change is necessary for all success, whether spiritual, social, physical, educational, intellectual or financial. To enhance all these areas of our lives, we must change the way we think, change what is important to us, and change our daily activities to achieve the desired outcomes. At times things may seem difficult, but nothing is impossible.

It's One or the Other — Notes

✦ What area in your life is causing you the *most* pain?
(Note which area and write it down—describe it.)

✦ Identify just one step you could take to ease at least some of that pain. Write it down.

✦ Do you think (or believe) this step (doing one thing
   to ease the pain) is more painful than the pain of not
   changing? If yes, why?

3

Believe It and Achieve It

*Obstacles are necessary for success ... as in all
careers of importance, victory comes only after
many struggles and countless defeats.*

– Og Mandino

It sounds simple, doesn't it? And it's true! What you believe you can achieve.

Mr. Mandino continued his thoughts by noting that each defeat sharpens your skills and strengths, your courage and your endurance, your ability and your confidence. So each obstacle is a comrade-in-arms forcing you to become better ... or quit!

Now, when I started my studies in my degree program, I was motivated by wanting a change from my job, and I was further motivated when I read Henry Ford's quote, "If you think you can or you can't, you are probably right." So, I was motivated to get started, but I had to believe that I could achieve my University degree while working full-time.

I also had a goal to write a book and I was inspired by other people accomplishing this and it motivated me to want to do the same.

Again, though, it was because I believed that I could write a book. I stayed motivated because the purpose of my book is to help other women and men achieve their goals and dreams while overcoming obstacles and challenges and oftentimes failing before being able to succeed.

A belief is nothing more than faith or passion that can provide direction and meaning in life. By trusting something which is true, your belief delivers a strong command to the mind to visualize what you are convinced will occur.

Og Mandino pointed out that each rebuff is an opportunity to move forward; turn away from them, avoid them, and you throw away your future.

Having a strong belief can be your most powerful tool in bringing great things into your life. A series of strong beliefs can empower you so you can achieve almost any goal that you set for yourself. Once you set your goal and you truly believe you can accomplish it, you will accomplish it. Throughout history, people who have had strong beliefs have accomplished things many people thought were previously impossible. These people believed it was possible and kept trying despite many unsuccessful attempts. They persevered.

Thomas Edison is known to have tried to create the electric light bulb more than 1,000 different ways. One of his financial backers is said to have asked: "Tom, why don't you quit? Can't you see this idea of yours is a failure?" Edison's response: "Every time it did not work I got feedback on how to make it better. I have now eliminated 1,000 ways it does not work and I get closer and closer to success." Every failure moved him toward to his goal. It's important to look at "failure" or "rejection" or "no" as a stepping stone to success.

Baseball and especially the recent home run quest by Mark McGuire and Sammy Sosa is a great example of failure. Both these men swung at the ball and missed it or hit it the wrong way about 100 times more often than they hit it the way they wanted. The average professional baseball player who earns $1 million per year fails to get on base 75% of the time. Seven times out of ten at bat, he walks back to the dugout having been unsuccessful at his job. Or was he? Baseball is a game of statistics, and so is life.

It is so easy to become dissuaded and discouraged when we do not succeed the first time we try something new. The learning experience of failing can bruise our ego. The projected pain of not looking good or feeling inadequate has stopped many efforts to even try again. I remember when I failed Linear Algebra, a course requirement for my University degree. I didn't understand it and found it extremely difficult. I should not have been surprised that I failed, and really I wasn't. I was more concerned about telling people that I failed and had to redo the course. But, I picked myself up again, hired a tutor, studied and wrote the exam again a few months later and passed.

I looked at this failure as a learning opportunity. How easy it would have been to just quit and give up and never reach my dream. I wasn't prepared to do that, I sucked it up and tried again. I developed a lot of character from that process and even today I'm inspired by my tenacity.

Do you remember when you first learned how to ride a bike? You didn't get on your bike thinking, "I'm never going to learn how to ride a bike!" If you did, then you should not have even bothered frustrating yourself. Sure, you may have fallen off your bike, got a few scrapes and bumps, but you still got back on. Soon enough, you learned how to ride your bike. You learned how to ride your bike, because others have and you believed you have the ability to do the same. Just believe you can do it and with determination you will do it!

Here is a motivational message that I believe will inspire you to go for your dream.

You Can Achieve Anything

You can achieve anything. There are no real barriers to your success. You must overcome any doubts you have about your ability. Your self-image prescribes the limits for your accomplishments. It prescribes the area of what is possible for you.

Don't be afraid of living. Your belief that life is worth living will help you create the fact around you. If you see yourself as prosperous, you will be. If you see yourself as continually hard up, that's precisely what you will be. You can never succeed until you believe you can succeed.

Everything is possible if you believe.

– Author unknown

Believe It and Achieve It — Notes

Here are some tips that will assist you on your journey to success:

1. *Have faith.* Someone said: "Walk by faith and not by sight." We don't have to know how we will accomplish

our goals and dreams; we just need to have faith that we will accomplish them.

2. *Trust.* Trust that there is a Divine Presence in your life that supports you in all that you do.

3. *Act as if.* If you are acting as if you are successful, it will motivate and inspire you to do the things, in order to have what you want.

4. *Expect success.* If you are planning to succeed and you are taking the action steps toward your goals and dreams, you will succeed.

✢ ✢ ✢

+ Remember when you first wanted to learn how to do something like ride a bike, ski, skateboard, cook, swim, use a cell phone or a computer?

+ When was this?

+ Before you started to learn, did you *really* believe you could do it? If you answered "no" what changed your mind (to "yes")?

+ What did you actually have to *do* to learn to ride a bike or any example you chose? List some of the steps.

+ How did you feel when you were successful?

IF YOU THINK YOU CAN
OR YOU CAN'T ...

> *You gain strength, courage and confidence by*
> *every experience in which you really stop to look*
> *fear in the face. You are able to say to yourself,*
> *"I've lived through this horror. I can take the next*
> *thing that comes along." You must do the thing*
> *you think you cannot do.*

– Eleanor Roosevelt

D o you realize that the only obstacle that can stop you from going after your dreams is you? Perhaps you have wanted to learn how to play a musical instrument, learn how to dance, or maybe you have always wanted to be a nurse. What was it that stopped you from pursuing your dreams? Did something tell you that you weren't good enough? Maybe you had people in your life that were jealous and felt threatened by someone who wanted to go after their dream.

It's exciting when you realize that no one and nothing has

power over you. Your success or failure is not up to fate and it's not up to luck. It's not up to your mom, your boss or your partner. The good news is it all begins and ends with you. When you take responsibility for your life and what you want to create in your lifetime, you will feel exhilarated! Simply put, if you think you can, you can; if you think you can't, you can't. What this means is that we must consciously decide that we will not settle! We must choose not to allow anyone or any circumstance to limit our lives and our dreams. Once I understood this, nothing could get in my way!

During my senior high school years, I had a dream of becoming a Physical Education teacher. It was ironic that I saw myself in this role, because I was overweight and overweight people often are unfit and not associated with people in this career. I wasn't athletic but I was active, and I just loved sports: baseball, hockey, curling, volleyball.

My mom didn't want me to go away to University. She preferred that I stay close to home and her dream was that I would meet someone, marry him and live across the road from their farm. I don't believe she didn't want me to do what I wanted, but I believe because of her own fears, she was unable to support and encourage me to go after my dreams.

My dad was always working on the land or fixing machinery, and I would talk to him about some things while he was working, but the conversation was broken up because of the distractions of whatever repair he was focusing. I didn't have much conversation with him about what I should do after high school. Perhaps I was worried that he would share Mom's feeling about me staying at home and farming, and I didn't want to hear that, because I knew I didn't want to be a farmer.

Both my dad and my mom didn't have much formal education—only up to a Grade 8 education. I believe they felt inferior to people who had many years of formal education. They felt formal education did not relate much to their belief that farming equated with honest, hard work.

When I was growing up, I had no one in my life to say to me, "Go for it! You can do it!" Unfortunately, there are so many of you out there who can relate to my experience, and I want to help you find your own strong inner voice that says "Yes! I can do this!"

It took me a few years to find my own inner voice.

One month before I finished high school, I traveled alone to the nearest city by bus to check out the University. I was 17 years old and had never been to the city. I stayed with a friend who lived near the University and the next day went and checked it out. I was overwhelmed by the size of the University and the buildings and everything in general. I was scared. I didn't know how I would manage in the city, let alone function in a University environment. All those thoughts clouded my vision of going to University to complete my dream of becoming a Physical Education teacher.

My own fears paralyzed me. I just kept thinking that I couldn't do it. On my return home to the farm, I decided that I just couldn't do it. I was so scared to live in the city and I wasn't confident in my ability to go to University, As a result of my lack of confidence, I gave up my dream of being a Physical Education teacher.

Instead, I found a job at a plywood mill where my hourly wage was $12.97 ... an incredible salary considered this was over 30 years ago! Although the wages were extraordinary, I knew almost immediately that I was not going to be working at the plywood mill till I retired. There were too many women there who had resigned themselves to that kind of life. I wasn't going to be one of them. *They* were not living their dreams!

I wanted more out of life—a career. So I decided to enroll in a 10-month clerk stenographer course. I saved the money I made at the mill, and I was very proud of myself for being able to fund my education. The clerk stenographer program turned out to be exactly what I needed at the time. It offered an opportunity to study and develop administrative skills. More important, it was something that I *believed* I could achieve, as it wasn't a big investment in time or money. I thought I could successfully complete the program and was committed to achieving that goal, and I did!

It always really bugged me that I chickened out of going to University. I felt that I had let myself down by allowing my own fear and lack of support to steal my dream. I viewed the completion of a degree program as a landmark of a great accomplishment and achievement. I also knew that having a University degree would open other employment opportunities. Since I was working in an administrative role and as part of a management team, I grew interested in the administration and management field. I explored different universities that would offer distance education courses, as that was my only option to study. By this time I had married and divorced. I had a year-old son, and I needed a job to support us; and I would need a means to pay for my education.

I was excited and nervous about committing to a long-term goal, and I questioned, "Who do I think I am to think I could complete a University degree?" and "How am I going to fit studying in with working full-time and raising a child?" All these questions raised fear and doubt. On exactly the same day that I was experiencing so much turmoil about whether to pursue the studies toward the degree program, I read this quote. It was on the front page of the weekly newspaper.

> *If you think you can or think you can't,*
> *you are probably right.*
>
> – Henry Ford

It's hard for me to describe how I felt when I read this. This quote was exactly what I needed to help me push past my fears of enrolling in the Bachelor of Administration degree. That very day I sent in my application, and I started my first course two weeks later.

It took me a very long time to finish my degree, and whenever I became discouraged about what seemed an insurmountable goal, I would remember Henry Ford's quote and it helped to inspire me to continue on, stay committed and finish what I set out to do. I was going to honor my self-promises and stay true to my goal. As I completed my courses, my confidence grew and I wanted to learn new skills.

Another skill which I wanted to develop was to be comfortable speaking to large groups.

I really admired people who could capture an audience and speak eloquently in public. Secretly, I would see myself in front of large groups delivering a message. In our community, there was a group of people who were starting up a Toastmasters club, and even though it scared me to death to speak in front of others, I desperately wanted to learn how to do it. More importantly, I wanted to face my fears and finally overcome the fear of speaking in public. I thought of Henry Ford's quote, "If you think you can or you can't, you're right!" That was what I needed to remind myself and to motivate me to go to the meeting. I didn't discuss going with my husband or anyone, I just went to Toastmasters.

I had just given birth to my second son two weeks prior to the first Toastmasters meeting, and I was self-conscious about the weight I had gained during my pregnancy: 61 pounds! I was extremely nervous and I thought I would faint when the chairperson called my name to do a table topic. I've heard the number one fear of people is to speak in public, and I believed it as I froze standing in front of the group! I felt like an idiot when I was asked to talk about a specific topic for two minutes and not a word came out of my mouth—my mind shut down when I stood up! As I sheepishly crawled back to my chair, I vowed that I would learn how to become comfortable speaking and I would not succumb to fear. Over the next year, I stuck with it and eventually mastered my fear. My confidence soared as I developed my speaking skills. I was so proud to overcome my fear of speaking in public.

F.E.A.R. is nothing more and nothing less than False Evidence Appearing Real

The following year, I was invited to do a presentation in front of 200 people. That was a most amazing feeling, and I felt fantastic after delivering a compelling message: "Empowerment: How to get what you want out of life."

Tom Russell said: "The key to independence is to *deny* the false self the agitation of dependency it craves. To get rid of the weasels of negativity, cease to feed them. Yes, the weasels will indeed protest. They will all assemble outside your door and bare their teeth yelling, 'Where's our food? How unkind of you, how selfish!'"

We all have negative "weasels" in our life. That lying voice that tells us we're not enough, we don't deserve success, abundance and prosperity. When these negative thoughts grow like weeds, we tend to over-think, which leads to debilitating self-doubt.

Soon we're wondering, "Am I incompetent in every area of my life?"

Michael Jordan said, "Some people get frozen by a fear of failure. They get it from their peers or from just thinking about the possibility of negative results. They might be afraid of looking bad or being embarrassed. I realized that if I was going to achieve anything in life, I had to be aggressive. I had to get out there and go for it. I don't believe you can achieve anything by being passive. I'm not thinking about anything except what I'm trying to accomplish. Any fear is an illusion. You think something is standing in your way, but nothing is really there. What is there is an opportunity to do your best and gain some success. If it turns out my best isn't good enough, then at least I'll never be able to look back and say I was too afraid to try. Failure always made me try harder next time."

To motivate yourself, write Henry Ford's quote on an index card, and post it where you see it all the time.

Whenever you are scared to do something, think of how you will feel if you don't do it. I believe you will feel empty and you will lose your zest for life. I see so many people who live a life of comfort and they watch what everyone else is doing. They don't particularly like their circumstance, and rather than change it, they conform to everyone else, rather than create. When you create, you get excited about your future and what you can do to make a difference.

I believe today, more than ever, we need to learn how to

handle fear. A life of fear brings with it anxiety, stress, frustration and anger which inevitably results in a loss of joy and hope. If we don't learn how to confront and control fear, we risk losing our emotional and physical health and ultimately the joy of living. Ask yourself, "What is it that I am afraid of doing?" Once you figure out what you really are afraid of, then instead of thinking to yourself "I can't do it," think "I really can do it!" And of course you can do whatever you set out to do. I know because I was you and if I can do it, so can you.

Quite frankly, I had moments of fear as I wrote this book. Some of my experiences are embarrassing, and I never revealed them before. I would think: "Who do I think I am? Who will read my book? Other people have had more life experiences, bigger challenges, larger obstacles and greater heartaches." So why did I share my story and write my book? Well, it was for someone like you, who can relate to living an ordinary life, trying to win typical life battles. I'm hopeful this will impact you and you will see how you can succeed by changing what you don't like, and maybe someday even writing about it too!

Lisa Jimenez, M.Ed., author of *Conquer Fear*, says we have to manage fear and change the relationship we have to fear. She goes on to say we can do this by neutralizing fear with its opposite: faith. We can cultivate faith. Faith is just like a muscle. The more you use it, the more you work it out, the stronger it gets. The stronger it gets, the more defined it gets and the more you see it alive in your life. And that's motivating!

Life is about growth. Get out of your comfort zone and go forward and face your fears. What you resist (fear) will persist. Fear is a fact not a force! Your fear should not immobilize you. Acknowledge your fear, face your fear and move on.

If You Think You Can or You Can't — Notes

Take five minutes ...

+ What is your greatest fear?

+ Now, take an index card and write: "If you think you can or you think you can't, you are probably right." (Henry Ford)

+ Affirm today: *I refuse to live engulfed by* FEAR!

+ Recall a time in your life when there was something you *really* wanted to do, something important to you like learn to drive a car, or ski, skateboard, cook a meal, use a computer, etc. Did you think "yes I can" or "no I can't"?

+ Why do you think you were able to drive a car or use a computer or whatever example you chose as an example?

You must persist

*The only difference between success
and failure is persistence.*

– Michael K. Byrd

Calvin Coolidge spoke about persistence. His words are often quoted appearing in framed form: "Nothing in this world can take the place of persistence. Talent will not; nothing is more common than unsuccessful people with talent. Genius will not; unrewarded genius is almost a proverb. Education will not; the world is full of educated derelicts. Persistence and determination alone are omnipotent. The slogan 'press on' has solved and always will solve the problems of the human race."

If it were not for my persistence, I would never have completed my University degree. It took me a long, long time to finish: twice as long as if I had attended on campus. When I started my degree, I was a single mom, working full-time. Four years after I started my degree I remarried, and a year later I had another baby, so I had a few distractions while pursuing my degree. Since the studies were through Distance Education, all I had was one call a week to my tutor and often that was to review assignments that were submitted. There was a small window of time that I could contact my tutor, and some weeks it was a challenge since I had to make sure I organized my family, especially my two little boys, as they often would still be awake in the evenings when the tutor support was available.

There were many assignments that I was required to complete before I could write the exam, which had to be scheduled six weeks in advance. I would do much of the work in the evening after my boys went to bed. The first time I brought my studies to work to get a bit more done during my lunch break, one of my co-workers complained to my boss, so he asked me not to bring my studies to the job. This was when I realized not everyone was happy about supporting my goals. However, none of that really mattered because I was not going to let anyone get in my way! I was determined to finish my degree despite anyone supporting me.

So between working full-time, caring for my two sons, cooking, cleaning, washing clothes, taking the boys to the park, coaching their little league softball, taking them skating and participating in community events, I carved out the time to study. I devoted my time to my family and had little or no time for my own activities. I no longer participated in a women's curling league or attending Toastmasters, both of which I really enjoyed. However, I made sure I worked out daily at 5:00 AM, before I had to get the boys up and ready for daycare. The only way I was going to succeed was by completing all the courses and it wasn't a matter of "if" I would obtain my Bachelor Administration degree, it was a matter of "when" I would achieve my goal. I was able to find a way to stay persistent.

Orison Swett Marden said: "There is genius in persistence. It conquers all opposers. It gives confidence. It annihilates obstacles. Everybody believes in a determined man. People know that when he undertakes a thing, the battle is half won, for his rule is to accomplish whatever he sets out to do."

Midway through my program, my neighbor and very dear friend, Sue, who was the same age as me, was diagnosed with breast cancer. It was devastating news. I spent many hours with her through her illness and then two years later, she passed away. It was such a sad time. Sue left behind her husband and two boys, ages three and five. Life was not fair.

I really felt like someone had pulled the carpet out from under my feet after Sue's death. I could have found every excuse to just throw the towel in on my studies; after all, I had two little boys and I was the same age as Sue. Who knew how long I would live? Did I want to spend my time studying when I could be having fun and creating memories for my boys? How important was it that I get my degree? I could have gone on and on to find reasons for not continuing my studies. Certainly, I did do some soul-searching after Sue's death, but then I made a decision: I would not let her death stop me from pursuing my dream. Sue knew I was pursuing a degree, and she was one of my biggest cheerleaders; she wouldn't have wanted to be the reason I gave up on my dream.

Deaths, tragedies and losses are all life's storms. Storms don't last. I believe they are there to test us: to see how badly we want to achieve our goals and dreams. I carried on with my studies and continued to persevere. Six months later, I attended my Convocation where I received my Bachelor of Administration degree.

T.D. Jakes, pastor, author, artist, entrepreneur, philanthropist and international influence, talks about people who arrive at success often don't feel like they have the taste of success. He says that this is because they worked so hard to achieve success and they are so exhausted from the journey. I could relate to this as I really couldn't believe that I had accomplished my goal, because the journey there was definitely not a paved road. It was full of potholes and speed bumps.

Maybe you have experienced a difficult time in your life, whether it was the pain of a loss or something else, and perhaps you feel it is still preventing you from being the best you can be. Decide today that you are a high achiever who will go for the gold and get it, and you will. When the challenges come, one can either be mastered by them or choose to be a victor over them. The person who is persistent is the one who continues to work even when it seems monotonous and the results can't be seen. Perseverance never gives up!

Here is something you can do to help keep you inspired to persevere. Look for successful people who have beaten the odds, who have overcome maybe the same past, maybe the same problems, and achieved what you want to achieve. Learn from them because if you apply what they did to your life, and you remain true to yourself, you will get where they are and have what they have: happiness and success. It is simply a question of learning their strategies.

William James said: "Most people never run far enough on their first wind, to find out what they have on their second." The race will be tough and you will face many difficult challenges. Remain steadfast on your journey. You will tire, but do not give up. You will struggle, but persevere. I challenge you to look inside yourself and find your second wind. Develop yourself and your skills to success.

You Must Persist — Notes

Here are some things to help you stay persistent.

1. Continually take action. It may be a small action step but if you do it daily you will accomplish enormous tasks.

2. Talk to yourself in positive, affirming ways. If you hear yourself saying things like "What's the point?" "I can't do this," or "I'll never get it," you must *immediately* say, "I can do this and I am achieving my goals." This must become a habit. The bottom line is if you don't believe in yourself, who will?

3. Have someone who supports you that you can call up who will tell you to keep going on no matter what. Make sure that this person doesn't tolerate your whining but does encourage you to keep on keeping on.

4. Review your plans, projects and dreams. Keep them in front of you.

5. Do *not* give up!

*   Were you able to ride the bike, or drive a car, or work the computer the very first time you tried?

*   Did you need to practice over and over, persisting, persevering, when you learned to ride a bike, drive a car or work the computer?

*   What did you do when you fell off your bike or could not do what you had to in one of the other examples?

✦ Write out or record why you want to achieve some goal you have for yourself (for a relationship, a job, education, success, health) and why this goal is very important to you.

Ask: "What if?"

Ask yourself: *What if…*

+ I fail

+ It is too hard

+ I can't handle the course load

+ My baby gets sick and I can't keep up

+ I don't feel like studying every night

+ I can't spend time with friends

+ I don't have the money to pay for the courses

+ I'm stuck and don't know the answer

And then ask: *What if I* SUCCEED?

Questions like these can help you move forward or they can stop you in your tracks. You really have to ask yourself another very important question: "How badly do you want it?" You just have to realize that your succeeding or not succeeding is a matter a choice. If you do nothing, you are making a choice.

I felt empowered when I asked myself "what if?" questions. I asked these questions when I was exploring furthering my education after my divorce. I thought, "What if I started studying toward a degree program, and finished the program? What opportunities would be available? How would I feel when I completed the University program?" When I started asking myself these questions, I started to see all the possibilities and it gave me so much energy. It made me feel alive.

If I didn't invest in further education, my future was pretty predictable. I would stay at the same job for 30 years, live in the same community and take the same route to work day in and day out. My face wrinkled just looking at this picture in my mind, because I didn't like the looks of it. I needed to obtain a University degree, as I saw it as a significant achievement and opportunity for career advancement.

Do you find yourself doing the same thing? You have a dream of doing something, but you are afraid to get started? Unreasonable thoughts attack our rational mind, inventing terrifying tales, which further justify or magnify our fears. When you hear yourself say or think, "But, what if?" you are caught in a common pattern of projecting fear and doubt into your dream. With this thinking, as you move toward your dream, you'll also move toward your fears and worst nightmares. With too much to risk, most of us give up or never even begin.

> *Your playing small doesn't serve the world. There's nothing enlightened about shrinking so that other people won't feel insecure around you.*
> – Marianne Williamson from *A Return to Love*

How I was able to confront my demons when I was feeling afraid was to draw a line across the center of a paper. On the top,

I wrote my dream in as much detail as possible. On the bottom, I wrote out my reality (about my dream) which included my fears, doubts and "but what ifs." Then I had to decide if I was more committed to my dream or to my fears. The idea of letting fear hold me hostage was disempowering, and when I fast-forwarded into the future as an old lady, I didn't want to have any regrets for not "going for it!"

While the idea of starting a business was frightening, at the same time it was exciting. I started to think about what impact I could have, how I could contribute to others and how I could create a certain lifestyle. I had to do the same exercise of asking the "what if" questions for starting my business as I did when I was pursuing a degree program. Because this exercise was so effective in the past, I knew it would help me overcome my fears of starting up my business.

I took a self-employment program, and since I was also just finishing up certification as a Registered Nutritional Consultant I decided to build a business in nutritional consulting. In class, I learned what was required to start a business and how to market a business. At the completion of the program, I achieved another dream: *Health Matters*, a business in nutrition consulting. I counseled people on how to live a healthy lifestyle through proper nutrition and exercise. I loved what I was doing because I loved to help people.

Within a year, though, I realized that not everyone wanted what I wanted in terms of health. There was no question that people wanted to be healthy and would seek my services, but they weren't willing to pay for the services. So, I realized I needed to re-evaluate what I was doing. I felt like a failure, and it did leave me insecure about starting something new. Although my business was not a success, I learned a lot from that experience. One of the things I learned was that while my business was a failure, I was not.

It's incredibly freeing to fail without considering yourself a failure or to be afraid and to risk any way. I hope you are inspired to be courageous, take risks and go for your dreams. These exercises will help you along the way.

Ask "What If?" — Notes

1. Separate your dreams from your fears.

2. Clearly recognize your doubts.

3. Identify if your obstacles require belief or strategies.

4. Prove that you believe in your dream by taking action.

5. Learn the necessary skills or get assistance.

✦   Look at your list of some of your special dreams which you are holding onto and which you have not realized.

✦   Make a list of as many of your fears as you can that you think about when you think about those dreams on your list.

✦   Are you willing to do something about the fears that stop you?

✦   Are you willing to allow your fears to *crush* your dreams?

ROADBLOCKS AND SPEED BUMPS

*When you face your fear, most of the time you will
discover that it was not really such a big threat
after all. We all need some form of deeply rooted,
powerful motivation—it empowers us to overcome
obstacles so we can live our dreams.*

– Les Brown

It took me many years to complete my degree program and I
had many challenges and obstacles: *roadblocks and speed bumps*.
My husband had a job that required lots of travel so he was
gone much of the time. It was a challenge to find time to study
while working full-time and taking care of two young boys. Since
my husband's job took him out of town frequently, I was often
managing without his assistance. There were many events that
caused me much heartache. It was a challenge to weather the
storms and win in life.

So what can be done when we are faced with challenges and
obstacles? How can we carry on? These challenges and obstacles

can be viewed as mere speed bumps rather than roadblocks to your dream. Joel Osteen said: "Every setback is a setup for a greater comeback." Your challenge is to focus on your future and push past those obstacles.

Some years back, my husband Bill lost his job when his position was eliminated after 17 years with the same company. It was a shock to him and me as well as our boys. It was especially devastating for our youngest son who was 10 years old at the time. He was freaked out and worried about our livelihood and questioned what we were going to do. He had grave concerns about how his world would change as a result, too. It definitely created anxious moments for me as well, but I was not about to "fall apart." I knew we were not immune to such an event and it was just another storm in life, and I certainly was conditioned to storms in life.

If I had shown any signs of despair when my husband lost his job, I wouldn't have been an anchor for him or my sons. I believed that my husband would find employment because he had just left a successful career, and that's what I told my sons. I remained hopeful and optimistic, even though it was difficult at times because it was a long wait. By focusing on the good, I believe my sons found comfort and assurance that all would be well. Now I'm amazed at how they take disappointments and challenges in stride.

Get excited about embarking on a new venture, your dreams and ultimately your success! Set your goals by taking time to plan and just get started. Success is taking action, and you will reach your goals even when the going gets tough. As I mentioned earlier, I believe challenges are to test us to see how committed we are to our goals and dreams. You have probably heard this cliché: *When the going gets tough, the tough get going.*

These roadblocks can actually become stepping stones to your success—by identifying which ones are holding you back from reaching your goals and diligently working to eliminate them.

Because there were no job opportunities for my husband, we relocated. That meant I gave up the career I was developing as a training consultant. I had little success in finding employment after we relocated, so I embraced the opportunity to explore starting a business. What I *really wanted* was to move from success in my career to *significance in my life*. I wanted to experience a life of prosperity and abundance by doing something that I loved and that made me feel like I was on vacation every day of my life. I also wanted to be financially independent, because it would allow me to make decisions that more closely aligned with my mission and values.

All this I knew, yet something was holding me back. It's true that I didn't have the emotional support to forge forward on my dreams, but that didn't seem to get in my way when I decided to pursue my Bachelor of Administration program or any other courses that I was interested in. This time was different, and as much as I could blame it on my family, I knew I was responsible for my lack of taking action.

It was my own limiting beliefs that held me hostage from my dreams. Limiting beliefs are the true killers, because they stop us from taking the actions we need to take to create our ideal lives. They stop us from living the lives we love!

So, what do I mean by limiting beliefs? Let me share this short story.

On May 6, 1954, something happened that changed the way millions of people think about human potential forever. You see for many, many years it was believed that no one could run a mile in less than 4 minutes. Thousands of runners had tried it but no one was able to do it.

Roger Bannister refused to accept this limiting belief. He told himself that it *is* possible, and that someone like him could do it. He planted beliefs (which were like seeds in his head) that he could run a mile in less than 4 minutes. And what do you think these seeds produced?

A result—a powerful result. Because, on May 6, 1954, Roger Bannister ran a mile in 3 minutes and 59.4 seconds.

But it gets better!

Because six weeks later John Landy from Australia ran a mile in 3 minutes and 58 seconds!

And it gets even better!

In the following ten years, many, many more runners broke this so-called "impossible" *4-minute mile* barrier. Why did this happen? Because Bannister shattered the belief that the 4-minute mile was impossible. And, when that belief fell ... the *less-than-4-minute mile* suddenly became possible.

Someone who achieves *big* results has *big* beliefs. Someone who achieves small results has small, limiting beliefs. So if you want to have big, unlimited beliefs then you need to plant such beliefs into your conscious and subconscious mind.

In order for me to achieve my goals and dreams, I had to believe that I had the ability; and I also had to believe I was worthy of my dreams and I deserved them. This is the number one issue I believe; people have the greatest problem not feeling good about themselves or about what they have to offer the world.

It doesn't matter where this limiting belief came from. All that matters is how to get rid of it and plant a new belief that says "yes I can do it" in its place. This is vital, because to be successful you have to be comfortable with who you are and what you have to offer the world.

No matter who says that:

- You can't make it
- You will never be anything
- You don't have what it takes
- You are not smart enough
- You are too old
- You can't make it because you are a woman or a single mom ...

... NOTE: If you are saying any of these things to yourself, consider getting a coach to overcome your inner doubts ...

... look up and say to people, circumstances and life: "That's not the way I see it." Now this is not going to come very easily at first. With coaching you too can overcome your inner doubts. It will help to adopt a "that's not the way I see it" attitude, which will help you feel empowered to go and live your dreams.

I know how challenging it can be to get past listening to what other people think or to feel pressured by others to do what they think is best for you. Perhaps you wanted to have a different career, but didn't act on your dream. Are any of these thoughts holding you back from pursuing your dream?

- I can't make a living doing something I really love.
- I'm too old.
- I can't go back to school.
- I'm just going through a silly phase of my life.
- My job dissatisfaction will pass.

This is your life! Your goals! Your success! Don't let your thoughts and limiting beliefs prevent you from living your best life. Go for your goals and dreams!

YOU ARE A WINNER!

Roadblocks & Speed Bumps — Notes

Understand that there will be challenges along the way, and here are some potential roadblocks to look out for:

1. *No clear vision.* The clearer your vision is of your definition for success, the faster you will achieve it. Those who succeed always see their success months and years before they live it. They have the ability to look ahead, see the future, imagine the good that can and will come from their lives, families and work. To not have vision is a tremendous roadblock. Sit down and work on seeing the future—and make it good!

2. *Fear of failure.* Don't let worry, fear or uncertainty hold you back from reaching your full potential. Fear is one of the worst enemies of success. When fear grabs a hold of you, it keeps you in bondage, and you will never be able to reach for your dreams. Confront your fears, see them for what they are, toss them to the side and pursue your dreams with relentless passion. Watch your words, too, and eliminate negative ones: no, never, can't, won't, maybe and if.

3. *Lack of perseverance.* Turn challenges into problems that need to be overcome. Don't let a challenge become a

stopping point on your path to success. Oftentimes the race is lost because the race is not finished. Success is often just around the sharpest corner or the steepest hill. Persevere. Keep going.

4. *Change.* You will have to make adjustments in your life to focus on reaching the success you want. For example: What current priorities on your time will have to be changed? Are you surrounded by people who can help you succeed? Are they quality people who will encourage you and strengthen you in your quest for success? If not, move on!

5. *Negative thinking.* Everyone has some self-doubt. What thoughts are you thinking? Are you saying, "I can never start a business." You need to be positive and optimistic by changing your thoughts. Say, "I am so happy now that I am my own boss."

6. *Lack of enthusiasm.* Quite frankly, what keeps most people from success is that they simply don't have the energy, or make the energy, to do what it takes to move to the next level. Don't get lethargic; get going!

7. *Procrastination.* You can have the best plan in the world, but if you don't take action on it you simply have a dream. Are you self-motivated, or do you need external motivation from someone else? Determine which method of motivation works for you. Take action.

8. *Making excuses.* Take personal responsibility for your success by eliminating excuses. Avoid blaming others

for your lack of effort. Accept responsibility for your life. You are responsible. When you accept that, you are on the road to success. Be sure to read Wayne Dyer's brilliant book, *Excuses Begone.*

9. *Learn from your mistakes.* Everyone makes them. Successful people learn extremely valuable life lessons from their mistakes.

✦ Write out how your life would be, what would it look like, how would it work as a "smooth-sailing road."

✦ What are some of *your* roadblocks and speed bumps that are stopping you from creating the life what you want?

✦ What can you do *today* to start removing those road-blocks?

4

You *Can* Do It

Do not wait; the time will never be "just right."
Start where you stand, and work with whatever tools
you may have at your command, and better tools
will be found as you go along.

– Napoleon Hill

You know that voice deep inside you—the one that says, "I've gotta get out of this relationship," "I've gotta get out of this job," "I've gotta give my dream a shot before it's too late!"

Every day and month and year that passes while you ignore that voice makes it harder to pretend that everything is fine. And then, finally, you've just gotta do it!

I first remember hearing that voice—and ignoring it.

Even while dating my boyfriend when I was 17 years old, I knew I didn't feel good about the relationship, but then I married him, thinking I would get that feeling and our relationship would improve. But it didn't. So then I thought it would get better when we had baby. After eight years, I came to the stark realization that

I could no longer live in an unhappy relationship. My inner voice said: "You can do it." Although I wanted to end the relationship, it was very difficult and very painful; it took a lot of courage to end the relationship.

A few years later … I heard the voice again …

One of the biggest reasons for enrolling in the Bachelor of Administration program was to give me other job opportunities. I couldn't see myself as an administrative assistant for the next 30 years, so I had to do something different if my life was to change. My opportunities to get an education were limited; I had to take distance education. I was scared about taking courses on my own, outside a classroom setting, but it was the only option as I had a baby to care for. I needed my job. All I heard was the voice deep down inside: "You can do it!" It helped to propel me to get a University degree.

That inner voice surfaced again …

My self-image was an ongoing challenge and I felt if I could lose some weight, it would change how I viewed myself. I struggled with my body image. I didn't feel good about myself and I was tired of always hearing myself complain. I was a pain to my family because I was always battling with my weight and it seemed that my weight challenge was my measure of happiness. I didn't like the amount of energy that I would waste complaining about my body and how I looked.

I learned of the Body-for-Life Challenge and was intrigued by the results. There was a substantial commitment to the 12-week challenge and I questioned whether I had the discipline. It involved restricted foods and limited amounts of food, as well as a well-designed exercise regimen. The voice inside said, "How badly do you want to change?" … and then, "You can do it!"

That inner voice kept screaming, "You can do it!"

After my nutrition consulting business failed, I worked for a privately owned training center as Manager, Student Services, and my job was to sell training programs to people who were looking to upgrade their skills. I wanted to quit. But I didn't have another job to go to. Then I asked myself: "What is this job doing for me, and what is this job doing to me?" At the same time that inner voice was screaming: "Quit! You can do it!" I prayed for the courage as I needed to get out of there. I listened to my inner voice.

> *Whatever you can do, or dream you can do, begin it.*
> *Boldness has genius, power and magic in it.*
>
> – Goethe

Sometime later, I attended a seminar where the speaker said, "Your dream loves you! Do you love your dream?" I got very emotional because I have always thought that there was more to life, and I wanted to experience it all. I wanted to be happy. It was at that seminar that I decided I was going to pursue my goals and dreams. No more excuses, only decisions. I made a decision to take action toward my goals and dreams. Since that day, I have not looked back. I have been reaching my goals and I am pursuing my dream. I've never been happier!

Abraham-Hicks in one their *Daily Quotes* available on their website (Abraham-Hicks.com) provided this insight.

> *Sometimes you walk into things that, if you were*
> *paying attention vibrationally, you would know right from*
> *the beginning that it wasn't what you are wanting. In most*
> *cases, your initial knee-jerk response was a pretty good*
> *indicator of how it was going to turn out later. The things*

that give most of you the most grief are those things that initially you had a feeling response about, but then you talked yourself out of it for one reason or another.

For whatever reason, we all have had to go through things in order to get where we are today. I realize that those challenges or obstacles had a purpose. I would not have grown had it not been for my challenges. I remember hearing a message at my church where the pastor said: "It is when you are in the valley that you learn, not when you're standing on a mountain top." Today, when problems or difficulties arise, I still don't like it, but what I've learned to do is try to see the opportunity in that problem. I'm reminded that these problems or challenges are just storms. If you ever think of a raging thunderstorm or a furious snow storm, they don't last, and that is like our challenges.

You Can Do It — Notes

+ Today, say to yourself at least ten times, "I can do it."

+ List all your accomplishments. Most of us cannot recall many of our accomplishments, so ask your family and friends and colleagues to "help you remember." One client listed "learning to walk"—she meant both times: first as a small child then again after a serious accident.

+ Don't forget to include accomplishments we often ignore such as getting your driver's license (which includes learning to drive), learning to use a cell phone, operate an ATM machine, play the piano or other musical instrument, sing, become a carpenter, use a computer, math skills (balance a checkbook, accounting), reading (technical reading), doing puzzles, learning to cook, knowing about wines, personal hygiene, fashion (how to dress for your work or for social occasions), meal planning and preparation, management skills (this is a big one), fishing, tennis or some other sport ...

+ What did you have to do to achieve even some of your accomplishments?

+ Are you beginning to detect a pattern yet?

ARE YOU READY TO SUCCEED?

As you look back on your life today what would you change? Anything? Everything? Have you lived a passionate adventure or have you lived life feeling pretty ho-hum?

In *A Return To Love,* Marianne Williamson says: "Our deepest fear is not that we are inadequate. Our deepest fear is that we are powerful beyond measure. It is our light, not our darkness, that most frightens us. We ask ourselves, who am I to be brilliant, gorgeous, talented, and fabulous? Actually, who are you not to be? You are a child of God."

She goes on: "It's not just in some of us; it's in everyone. And as we let our own light shine, we unconsciously give other people permission to do the same. As we're liberated from our own fear, our presence automatically liberates others."

The great tragedy of life is that so many people go to their graves with their lives unlived. They had dreams that they never acted on. They lived the sort of life that they felt was expected of them. They were so busy trying to please other people that they had no time for their own happiness.

This you must know: there are people who love you, care about you and respect you, but until you learn to love and care about yourself, until you learn to respect yourself, you will never truly accept the love, care and respect of others.

Do you know that we weren't put on earth just to make money and raise a family? We all have our own individual callings, but we have to listen to them and choose to be bold and courageous enough to take action based on them. Everyone is here to serve in some way.

You can create your inspired life ... you just have to choose it. Ask yourself "What one thing could I do today that would make a positive difference in my life and the lives of those around me?"

Now, I've heard many of you immediately say "*me*?" "Me? Little old me? How can I make a difference? I am not important, or powerful or rich, I am just an ordinary person struggling to make a living. How can I make a difference?"

Well the very first thing that you should do is to change your attitude about yourself, because until you think that you are special, you won't be. Until you can recognize the magnificent potential that is locked up inside you, strapped down by all those negative beliefs, you will not be able to release it and live to your full potential.

You have the greatest power of any living thing on this planet: you have the power of choice. You have the power to choose how to behave, what to say and when to say it. You have the power to control your attitude. You have the power to make a difference

Choose to make difference. Choose to look for the positive in all things; if you really can't find something positive to say or do, then do and say nothing.

Realize that you do not have to do something earth-shattering to make a difference. It's the little things you do every day that often have the greatest impact. A smile, a friendly word, a compliment, a helping hand, a sympathetic ear—these are the things that you can do every day. Learn to get your satisfaction from helping others to feel better about themselves and their lives.

Pastor Robert H. Schuller says, "When you were born, you were given the gift of life. Make today the day that you accept that gift. Realize that you were designed for accomplishment, engineered for success and endowed with the seeds of greatness."

Each moment is a new opportunity with new choices.

My burning desire has always been to make a difference: to give back. My measure of success is when I am helping people, because it makes me feel good. I believe my purpose is to help people. Every day I make it a goal to do something nice: one random act of kindness. I have fun with it because I never know who I will meet. My ultimate goal is to build a foundation, and my passion is to support and empower women and men to go and live their dreams. I want to live a legacy and leave a legacy.

W. Clement Stone said, "Whatever the mind of man can conceive, it can achieve." What is it that you would you like to achieve? How would like to be remembered?

I especially like this poem by Robert H. Schuller:

I will! I am! I can!
I will actualize my dream.
I will press ahead.
I will settle down and see it through.
I will solve the problems.
I will pay the price.
I will never walk away from my dream
until I see my dream walk away:
Alert! Alive! Achieved!

Are You Ready to Succeed? — Notes

Here are some questions I asked myself before I made some choices about how I wanted to live my life. You may find them helpful too.

1. Where do I see myself in five years?

2. Will I be happy?

3. What would I like to do differently?

4. Do I want more money? How much?

5. How will I spend the money?

6. How do I want to be remembered?

7. How will I accomplish this?

8. Who can support me?

Are you ready to SUCCEED?

+ What is the *first* thing that comes into your mind when you read that sentence?

+ Where will I be one year from today? In three years? Five? (Consider work, home, relationships.)

+ In the five-year view: Will I be happy?

+ What will happen if I don't make changes in my life?

SINGLE, AND YET NOT ALONE

In the long run we shape our lives and we shape
ourselves. The process never ends until we die.
And the choices we make are ultimately our
own responsibility.

– Eleanor Roosevelt

Even though we think we know what we want, it does not nec-essarily mean life won't give us more than we bargain for—good or bad! It is important to understand and accept that, although we each have certain values that we want to create in our life, our values will shift and change. The important lesson is to constantly communicate your goals and dreams to the people in your life. This is especially true if you plan to marry.

In my mind, I knew what I wanted, and I just believed other people in my life would also want what I wanted and everything would fall into place. Unfortunately, I learned differently, and as a result, my decisions created much heartache. You may be able to relate to this: You wake up one day and realize that because you were so focused on what you wanted, you didn't really pay attention to what the other person in your life wanted or didn't want. Or if you were like me, you just thought that even though you knew what the other person wanted or didn't want, he would come around and see things your way or they wouldn't affect your relationship. Everything would sort itself out and be just fine. But then, all of a sudden, you realize that everything really is not fine!

Right at the outset, I knew my relationship with my boyfriend, then husband, was wrong. But instead of getting out, I got further into the relationship.

After a year being in the relationship, it didn't feel good and it was going nowhere. I didn't want to hurt his feelings, and I hated myself for doing things I didn't want to do. I really didn't want to be with him, but I felt sorry for him. I hated that he expected me to do things that were against my values (premarital sex), but I wasn't strong enough to stop so I continued to do those things and just felt guilty. I was so confused. I didn't feel I had anyone to talk to, and I was scared to tell how I felt and embarrassed to share what I had done.

I felt trapped and I didn't have the confidence to tell him myself that he pulled me down. So instead I fought with the voice inside that said, "You can't settle for this relationship," and just resigned myself to believing that in time things would change, and I would feel differently and learn to love him. My self-image was at an all-time low, and I just thought I might as well take what I've got. After all, who else would want me?

I didn't know who to please and I didn't know what I wanted. In the end, I made the worst mistake a woman can make. I settled.

For the next few years, our relationship was up and down:

sometimes okay, sometimes not. We had different interests. He liked to camp in remote areas and hunt too. I don't like to be around people killing animals. I liked to stay at recreational camp sites. I loved to play ball, skate, walk and run, and he hated exercise. I loved to be around people, he didn't. I loved social events. He found excuses not to attend. I would go out of my way to help people, but he wanted people to come to him if they needed his assistance. I was an extrovert, he was an introvert. It was not healthy for either one of us.

After being married for about five years, I became pregnant. I was thrilled! I didn't tell my husband for three months, because I was scared that he might not be too thrilled. Not only was my husband *not* happy about me being pregnant, he was mad. I thought he would feel differently about having children when he found out I was expecting his child, but I was wrong. He did try to get used to the idea and seemed to accept our son's safe arrival; however, he was not comfortable taking care of him and was extremely nervous if our son fussed. He would never take our son out with him, for fear that if he fussed he wouldn't know what to do.

Over the next six months, I realized I needed to make a decision about whether to stay in the relationship or not. I was not happy, and it was not healthy for my son. I thought things would change, but I knew that in order for things to change, I had to change.

It was so hard to live in an unhealthy environment where I felt like I had to pretend to be happy. I can remember thinking that I should be happy: my life was comfortable. It would be easy, I tried to reason, to just continue to keep trying to conform, by doing what was pleasing to my husband. I thought about how easy it would be to settle for a life of unhappiness, rather than to be on my own. After all, if I looked back on the 10 years in that relationship, it really hadn't changed. The only thing that changed after all that time was I had the courage to get out ... once and for all. In the end, my husband left.

Going through a divorce was an upsetting time, but at the same time it felt so good to be out of the relationship. Certainly there were different challenges, as I was granted sole custody of our 18-month old son, and being a single mother was a challenge. Many of my friends abandoned me. Some of my friends' husbands, and even some family members, would not let their wives continue their friendship with me, and I learned later that it was because their husbands were afraid that their wives would be influenced by my decisions. It was a very lonely time.

Lisa Nichols of *The Secret* says it best: "It's important to know who you are bringing into the relationship, and that person is *you!*" Neale Donald Walsh in his book, *Who is God?*, discusses relationships and how important it is that we enter into the relationship interdependently and not look for the other person's approval. He also says it is important that you know who you are before entering into a relationship and to be happy and accept who you are.

Certainly, I am not proud of the fact that I brought a child into an unstable relationship. I guess I was selfish. I needed that baby to help me to feel less alone and to get out of that relationship. With my child, I didn't have to do it alone. Now I was single, but not alone.

Unfortunately, I am not unique in making this mistake. Many other women, and you may be one of them, share a similar experience. You may be in a similar situation in an unhappy relationship. You may be asking yourself, "Should I stay or should I go? What is the relationship doing *for* me and what is the relationship doing *to* me?" I believe we need to be true to ourselves and if there is something or someone holding you back from living your best life, then you need to consider making some changes.

Even though my husband decided to move out, and even though living through the ending of this relationship was certainly one of the hardest things I have ever had to do, the whole experience taught me an invaluable lesson. I learned that I am a strong, independent woman who will not tolerate a life of always conforming and compromising. I may not have known exactly what I wanted then, but I sure knew what I didn't want.

Being a single mom allowed me to see how I was responsible for my choices, and it also showed me that even though I made a wrong choice, I could wake up and greet the morning as the next chapter of my life. It has also given me the opportunity to share with so many other women my experience and inspire them to go on to create something better for themselves and their children. Charles "Tremendous" Jones said: "Things don't go wrong and break your heart so you can become bitter and give up. They happen to break you down and build you up so you can be all that you were intended to be." Then you can be *you*.

Single and Yet Not Alone — Notes

+ Are there some choices you have made in the past that are *not serving* you anymore?

+ What *new* choice or choices can you make today that will better serve you today?

+ How do think you will feel after making that change?

You can't do it alone

*All of the great achievers of the past
have been visionary figures.*

– Bob Proctor

Reaching your potential takes hard work, commitment and discipline. The good news is you don't have to do it all alone! If you truly want to live to your potential, you need to work with someone who can help you achieve results.

Great achievers, the men and women who projected their ideas into the future, almost always talked about their ideas with others whom they trust. They thought of what could be, rather than what already was, and then they moved themselves into action to bring these things into fruition. That always took collaboration.

For years I tried to figure out what I wanted to be, do and have in my life, and I bought so many books to help give me clarity. I was inspired by people's success and I was highly motivated to succeed, but at the completion of each book, all I had was knowledge.

I needed to put that knowledge into action, but I didn't know how. I was happy for other people's success, but I was discouraged because of my lack of progress. In fact, I was stuck! If I wanted to move from mediocrity to greatness, I needed a coach. I needed someone to help me find clarity in what I wanted and I needed the support.

For most of us, extra support *can* make all the difference in the world. Having a coach gives you the vehicle for accelerated accomplishment of your goals. In this challenging world it is easy to get off track with what is most important to you. A coach keeps you focused, on purpose, and works with you to redefine goals and dreams.

In the 21st century, coaching is no longer a luxury but a necessity! People dedicated to self-improvement work with different coaches throughout their lifetime and experience a higher level of living as a result. Coaching also creates a bridge that takes you from where you are now to where you want to be. Just as top athletes have coaches to bring out their best performance, coaching helps clients build on their own inner strengths. Your coach is invested in your success and provides insight, structure and encouragement for increased effectiveness and fast improvements.

Brian Tracy spoke of the potential of the average person as being like a huge ocean unsailed, a new continent unexplored, a world of possibilities waiting to be released and channeled toward some great good.

There are obvious benefits to becoming someone who is committed to lifelong improvement: you feel better about yourself, you are more willing to take risks and accept challenges, and you live to your potential. It is in the reaching that you find out who you really are and all you are capable of. It is exciting because there is always something new you can learn.

We are all works in progress, living examples of art. Continuous self-improvement keeps you turned on and tuned into life. And as a result, you evolve as a human being. You make a difference in the world by being the best *you* that you can be. Your best inspires others to be their best, and the very nature of humanity becomes improved.

Simply talking to a non-judgmental third party can do wonders for you. When people face problems, they are often too embarrassed to ask for help. They may not want their friends or family to know they are struggling with something. This can lead to further feelings of isolation and depression. A personal coach is there to listen and help you find solutions for your problems.

Working with a personal coach is actually more affordable than you think. Most offer free consultations. It is important for you and your potential coach to get to know each other; after the initial consultation, you can decide if this coach is the right coach for you. Likewise, the coach can tell you openly and honestly if they can help you. If they can't, they will refer you to someone who can.

Think about how great it would be to have someone on your side, rooting for you, giving you honest feedback and helping you achieve new goals. These are benefits of having a personal coach.

1. *Setting goals.* One of the primary focuses of a coach is that of setting and reaching goals. One of the main reasons people have difficulty manifesting success in their life is simply because they have no idea what their own idea of personal success really is. It's like a businessman with no business. Without any source of direction, how can a person expect any quantifiable results? A coach can ask questions to isolate what is most important to their client

and once that goal or goals are isolated, then the coach can help "reverse engineer" that goal to come up with a workable action plan.

2. *Clarity.* A coach can help you clarify your present condition and your future directions.

3. *Action.* Success rarely manifests itself. Knowledge and ideas are great to have, but they also do not manifest success in and of themselves. Action is what creates success in life. The reason many intelligent and knowledgeable people do not experience the level of success that they desire is because they are slow to act on or apply the knowledge they have. A coach can help their client make decisions much more quickly, reduce costly delays and provide better quality action with less risk.

4. *Motivation.* Even the best experts in the world utilize coaches, consultants and personal advisors because there is a strong psychological factor of accountability when another person has oversight on your progress. Actors, models, even bodybuilders have personal trainers who make sure they are keeping up on their program to reach their intended goals and this acts as a powerful motivating force for them. It's the same with life coaches. They motivate their clients towards their goals and they make them accountable for maintaining their program and sticking to it.

5. *Support.* A coach will listen to your story without evaluating, criticizing, judging or offering solutions. They will

lend their support to you through the toughest of times as well as the best of times.

6. *Overcoming challenges.* We all face certain roadblocks in our lives that need to be overcome for us to achieve measurable success. A coach can help their client brainstorm for possible solutions to complex challenges that need to be dealt with.

7. *Life balance.* A coach can improve the ratio of work versus play in your life to achieve an optimal balanced ratio of both. This will lead to reduced stress levels and a better quality of life.

8. *Consulting.* Most coaches specialize or have expertise in specific areas such as entrepreneurship, health and fitness, or stress management. This expertise can be invaluable to their client who requires it.

9. *Confidentiality.* Although coaching is not therapy or counseling, ethics dictate that the same rules of client confidentiality apply to coaching sessions. Therefore, what is discussed between a client and a coach is strictly confidential.

When you are looking for a coach or mentor, seek out someone who has already accomplished what you are trying to achieve. A coach who is experienced in what you wish to achieve will be able to share with you insights and strategies you can use to get results. They can give you decades of wisdom in each coaching session.

Hiring a coach was one of the best decisions I made. With the help of my coach, I have been able to accomplish many goals and one of them was writing this book. I am now working toward bigger goals and I am visualizing my dreams coming true. My investment in hiring a coach has come back tenfold. I have accomplished so much since working with a coach, and I absolutely believe that I would still be stuck if I hadn't hired a coach.

You Can't Do It Alone—Notes

If I could support you and help you in accomplishing your goals, is that something you would like to talk about? Here are some ways I can help:

✦ Help you set goals and help you reach your goals.

✦ Help you clarify your present condition and your future direction.

✦ Help you make decisions much more quickly, and reduce costly delays; provide better quality action with less risk.

✦ Help motivate you towards your goals with accountability so you will maintain your program and stick to it!

✦ Help you brainstorm for possible solutions to complex challenges that need to be dealt with.

You can contact me by telephone at 701-205-4071 or e-mail: julie@expectsuccessbeunstoppable.com

5

Attitude is Everything

*Your mental attitude is something you can control
outright and you must use self-discipline until you create
a positive mental attitude—your mental attitude attracts
to you everything that makes you what you are.*

– Napoleon Hill

Our attitude is the mental filter through which we see the world. We can see things as positive or negative and we can perceive these events or circumstances as good or bad. We can choose how we see things. Attitude affects belief and attitude activates all of the other success principles. Some of these principles are persistence, courage, energy and enthusiasm. There is a correlation between energy and enthusiasm—energy sells when we have a good attitude and it attracts the people you want in your life. Spiritual growth comes with being positive and open, and when you are optimistic it creates possibilities.

The very first time I became aware of how my attitude had an effect on me and my surroundings was after my accident. I was at the hospital, and as I wheeled myself into the hospital lounge, two old guys laughed at me. These old guys really boosted my spirits, because they made me realize that I had *survived* an accident, and it could have been much worse. They made me realize that I should be glad to be alive.

> *Your living is determined not so much by what life*
> *brings you as by the attitude you bring to life; not*
> *so much by what happens to you as by the way*
> *your mind looks at what happens.*
>
> – Lewis L. Dunnington

I could have adopted the attitude of "why me?" and become a victim of circumstance, and maybe I'd have people around to support me and feel sorry for me. Instead I chose not to be a victim and focused on being able to walk again.

Those two old guys (I can still see them with their toothless grins!) helped me to see that I could create or paint a life of how it can be, rather than how it was. My circumstance was temporary; it was an event and not a show-stopper!

As Benjamin Disraeli pointed out, we are not creatures of circumstance; we are creators of circumstance.

Years later I read an article by Chuck Swindoll on "Attitude," and I have it in my office, hanging on the wall, where it serves as a constant reminder that I have the ability to choose, and my choices will affect my quality of life. This is how he views attitude:

> *The longer I live, the more I realize the impact of atti-*
> *tude on life. Attitude to me is more important than facts. It*
> *is more important than the past, than circumstances, than*
> *money, than education, than failures, than successes, than*

what other people think or say or do. It is more important than appearance, than giftedness, or skill. It will make or break a company—a church—a home.

The remarkable thing is that we have a choice every day regarding the attitude we embrace for that day. We cannot change our past. We cannot change the fact that people act in a certain way. We cannot change the inevitable.

The only thing we can do is play on the one string we have, and that is our attitude. I am convinced that life is 10% what actually happens to me and 90% how I react to it.

So it is with you and me. We are all in charge of our attitudes. This has been an invaluable lesson to me, and I can't say that it happened overnight, but once I changed my attitude, I was a far happier and more productive person. I believe everyone can benefit by understanding this simple message.

The next time you feel compelled to "react" to some circumstance in your life, really think about how it could affect your life. Here are a few everyday situations that you may encounter. How would you react? You get to choose!

+ You are driving to work in the morning and someone cuts you off.

+ Your doctor's appointment is 30 minutes behind schedule.

+ It is 6:00 AM and your hot water tank just broke!

+ You get a call to pick up your son, because he has had too much to drink.

Decide when you get up in the morning that you are going to start a new day in a new way! "If you don't like something, change it. If you can't change it, change your attitude. Don't complain," says Maya Angelou.

Think about this. Each day the sun rises. It doesn't know about your life, it does what it is supposed to do each day. It doesn't say to the earth, "You owe me!" All the sun does is rise and create a world of beauty. Imagine if you were like the sun. You have a choice, and only you can make the choice as to what type of day it will be. If you wish for negative things, expect them. It says in the Bible, Matthew 7:7, "Ask and it shall be given to you." If you wish for a day full of excitement and challenge, it will be given to you. *You* make the call!

If you are tired of a mediocre life, decide that you will no longer be a victim. Make new decisions, believe you deserve it and go and be the sun: *shine*!

The following is a poem that Irby Stewart, delivered at a presentation at our workplace several years ago. He was the epitome of a positive attitude. At the time I met him, he was preparing to celebrate his 65th birthday the following month by rollerblading approximately 500 miles. What an inspiration! All because of his attitude and belief!

IF

If you think you are beaten, you are.
If you think you dare not, you don't.
If you like to win, but think you can't
It is almost certain you won't.
If you think you'll lose, you're lost.

For out of the world we find,
Success begins with a fellow's will—
It's all in the state of mind.
If you think you are outclassed, you are.
You've got to think high to rise.
You've got to be sure of yourself before
You can ever win a prize.
Life's battles don't always go
To the stronger or faster person,
But sooner or later the person who wins
Is the person who
THINKS THEY CAN!

– Irby Stewart

Attitude is Everything — Notes

To achieve a positive attitude, you must take physical, verbal and mental actions. Here are some ways to help:

1. *Understand you always have a choice.* Attitude is a choice and most people select from the negative column. Reason? It is more natural to blame and defend than it is to admit and take responsibility.

2. *Admit it is the fault of no one but yourself.* The more you blame others, the less chance you have to think positive thoughts, see a positive solution, or take positive action toward solution. The opposite of blame is responsibility. Your first responsibility is to control your inner thoughts and thought direction.

3. *Watch your words.* Do you look at the glass as half full or half empty? They are just words, but they are a reflection of how your mind sees things and an indication of how you process thoughts. Avoid confrontational and negative words. The worst ones are: why, cannot, will not and should.

4. *Choose your news.* You get bombarded every day with a news media that believes in the mantra, "If it bleeds, it leads!" followed by commercials designed to make you feel better. Our media strives to ramp up your feelings of anxiety by highlighting horrific stories and follows them with advertising that helps you to buy comfort food or medications to relieve the pressures of everyday life. Unplug yourself from this negative imagery. Find alternative sources to keep yourself up to date with the day's events, such as public radio or print news. It's easy to choose what to listen to and read.

5. *Surround yourself with positive people.* Family, friends and co-workers who have a negative view about life can make it hard for you to maintain your positive attitude. These people can drain you mentally and physically. Wherever possible, avoid them or at least limit your contact with them. If you cannot avoid them, don't get drawn into lengthy gripe sessions. Listen empathetically and turn the conversation to a more positive topic as soon as you can. On the other hand, positive people can enhance your life and help to keep you upbeat and with a good outlook on your world.

6. *Begin every day with 15 minutes of positive thoughts.* If you fill your mind with positive thoughts, you'll have a larger library of positive thinking to pull from when your day might not quite go as planned. Read an inspirational book or listen to CDs of positive thinkers.

7. *Count your blessings.* Write out a list of all the things you have to be grateful for and that will make you feel good and put you in a positive mindset.

8. *Fill your mind with positive thoughts.* Here is one positive thought sent to me from my publisher to get *you* started:

> *Today is not a gift.*
> *It is an achievement.*
> *You are here today.*
> *That is an accomplishment!*
>
> – Author unknown

9. Take responsibility for everything that happens in your life ... good and bad.

10. Do you want some ideas on how to surround yourself with positive people? Ask me how by sending an e-mail to julie@expectsuccessbeunstoppable.com.

How do you look at the glass?

Stories can often carry a lesson better than any lecture. This is the situation when we read Thich Nhat Hanh as he relates a story with an important message. When you plant lettuce, if it does not grow well you don't blame the lettuce. You look for reasons it is not doing well. It may need fertilizer, or more water, or less sun. You never blame the lettuce. Yet if we have problems with our friends or family, we blame the other person. But if we know how to take care of them, they will grow well, like the lettuce. Blaming has no positive effect at all, nor does trying to persuade using reason and argument. That is my experience. No blame, no reasoning, no argument, just understanding. If you understand, and you show that you understand, you can love, and the situation will change.

Look at the glass on the table in front of you. Is it half full or is it half empty? Now, do you realize that it is entirely for you to decide what the answer to this question is going to be? The choice is yours. So, the very same reality can be seen in totally opposite ways: in a positive way and in a negative way.

My coach often reminded me: "There are no mistakes in the

universe." During times when things are not going well, this statement can be difficult to swallow. As you read this, you can probably quickly remember a time or times when you have experienced challenges and your unwillingness to face them is equal to the degree you experienced pain—as a result of sickness, injury or even death of a loved one. You may ask, "How can there be no mistakes, when I am so mad or sad about losing someone I loved?"

The worst thing a person can do is to become a victim of their circumstances. Sure, we may not be able to undo what has happened. We don't have to *just accept* what has happened, but we do get to choose how we respond. Women, especially women over 40, are often told to stay calm or to bottle up their feelings. This is disempowering and it helps create those "victim" feelings. Instead, when you don't like how something is in your life, express it! Get mad if that's the appropriate response. Go ahead. It's healthy to express emotions. But it is important to be in control of the way you express your emotions. So when you get mad, put a deadline on how long you are going to stay mad. It really does not serve anyone to get caught up in your emotions so that it paralyzes you to move forward in your life.

I've learned and accepted that no one owes me anything, and neither am I immune to any obstacles, challenges, tragedies or losses. Throughout my years, I have experienced many disappointments, sorrows, accidents and deaths, and there was much pain around these events. Through this pain, though, I believe my character developed and strengthened. By focusing on what I do have and being grateful, I can show you how I was able to overcome my challenges.

The injuries I sustained in my car accident eliminated my participating in many activities; I loved to play ball, go for walks, skate and curl. But, remember the lessons in the wheelchair? Instead of focusing on what I couldn't do, I reminded myself that I was so lucky to even survive the car accident even if I was in a wheelchair the rest of my life. I looked at the glass as half full, rather than half empty. Although I still experience discomfort in my ankles, I enjoy daily workouts and I go for shorter walks. Each time I am walking, I look at my legs and marvel at how I can move after such a horrific accident. Although the doctors have told me that I may require a wheelchair in my senior years, I don't dwell on it; I can walk today and that is all that matters.

Another time I looked at the glass as half full was when I was going through my divorce. Although I knew that it was the right decision to be a single mom, it was a big responsibility to raise my son on my own. It would have been easy to feel sorry for myself and play the victim role, but I wouldn't allow myself to do that. Instead of the glass being half empty, it was half full. I had a job so I could support myself and my son, I had excellent care for my son and I had a reliable vehicle. I felt fortunate.

I can remember my older sister saying, "I don't know how you can go to work when you are going through a divorce!" I recall saying, "I can't afford not to go to work and be positive; otherwise I would lose my job!" I couldn't blame anything or anyone for the choices I made, and I sure wasn't about to crumble in a heap and give up because of a failed relationship. I took responsibility for my decisions.

Yes, there are times when something is legitimately not our fault. Blaming others, however, keeps us in a stuck state and is ultimately rough on our own self-esteem.

– Eric Allenbaugh

I've had many disappointments, obstacles, challenges, accidents, tragedies and losses in my life: emergency surgery, a car accident, jealous friends and co-workers, demanding bosses, lost jobs, divorce, being a single mom, failed businesses, health scares, challenges with kids, and friends and loved ones who died.

But, my list is not unique. We've all experienced these things or something like them. These events are all part of life, but they are not show-stoppers. Robert H. Schuller said, "It's important to remember that the walk of faith is designed to serve God's cause in his Kingdom. We are invited to be soldiers in God's army—not tourists on an around-the-world trip." I have learned to look at the world in a different way. Look at the glass as half full: try to find out that positive side and turn it into something good. At first you might literally have to dig it out, but after some time it automatically appears to you. In fact, you eventually only see the good side.

Napoleon Hill, author of the classic book, *Think and Grow Rich*, struggled for 20 years to write the definitive guide to success, but he experienced poverty, his life was threatened, his backers were murdered, he suffered from bouts of hopelessness, and his family suffered beyond all understanding.

One thing that stood out in Hill's life story was his ability to turn the negative into the positive. He always looked for what some people call that silver lining in the dark cloud.

We can all do this: if someone has wronged you, ask yourself, "How can I turn this into something good?" Now, this goes against what most people ever even attempt to try. The whole idea of taking whatever happens to you and turning it into something good seems, at first glance, preposterous.

But this also seems to be a key to success.

Today, I look at the glass as half full, and I'm turning all of my life's obstacles and challenges into something good. I'm sharing my story in order to help other people who may be experiencing similar situations. Taking the so-called negative experiences in life and turning them into something good.

You have the ability to do this. It's a choice. No matter what happens, take a breath and ask, "How can I turn this into something good?"

In good times and bad times, having a positive attitude has given me the ability to see good in all situations. This isn't always easy, but I've learned it is important to be thankful for all bad situations in my life, in order to appreciate the good.

How Do You Look at the Glass? — Notes

✦ Think of a time when you experienced an accident, a loss, tragedy or any other unwelcome event.

✦ How did you respond?

✦ Did anything good come out of it?

Inspiration versus motivation

Motivation is like bathing … It may not last,
but it's still a good idea now and then.

– Jim Cathcart

There is a difference between inspiration and motivation. Motivation will get you excited and it will help you take action. Inspiration will keep you self-motivated.

The challenge around motivation is staying motivated. You need to listen to motivational CDs or read books that keep you motivated in order to work toward your goals. Daily motivation is like taking a shower. It wears off, so you have to make a habit of doing something each day to keep you motivated. If you spend even 20 to 30 minutes a day reading or listening to something motivational, you will see how you can make progress, stay in activity and reach your goals.

Inspiration, on the other hand will keep you self-motivated. Inspiration can come from many sources, and often it is through other people's success stories. There are so many stories of people and how they have overcome challenges. Their success was not overnight either! Take a look at Thomas Edison, who tried 1,000 times before his invention of the light bulb came to fruition? He was a big joke, too! How about Abraham Lincoln? He had many roadblocks and major bumps on the road before becoming president. He was unsuccessful getting elected a number of times before he finally got into office at age 52. Other celebrities like Michael Jordan got cut from the high school basketball team! Find people who inspire you. Read their story and follow their lead!

You may relate to my story about my weight challenges which started as a teenager; maybe you, too, have battled with weight gain or struggled with maintaining your weight. Even today, my weight fluctuates, and if I didn't take pride in my appearance, I could easily let it slide.

I didn't know what really big weight issues were until I became pregnant! With my first pregnancy, I gained a moderate 20 pounds, but with my second pregnancy, I gained 61 pounds. Ouch! I hated going to the clinic for my checkups, because one of the nurses was very disgusted each time she would weigh me. She would suggest that I was out of control with my eating. I swear! All I had to do was look at the fridge and I would gain weight!

After my first son was born, all I lost was his birth weight, which was 9 pounds, 5 ounces. I only lost 8 pounds after my second son's birth! So many people told me that I would lose most of the weight, because it was all water! Not true! I was overjoyed with the birth of my second son, but I was very depressed about my weight gain. It didn't matter if I nursed; I still didn't shed much weight. I was motivated to lose weight, so I started to work out a few months later and that helped a bit, but I didn't get the results I wanted. However, I found out that I loved lifting weights and raising my heart rate released the endorphins, which made me feel amazing. So even though I made slow progress, I focused on feeling good.

A few years later, I was introduced to a 12-week Body-for-Life Challenge, a weight-loss program that was developed by Bill Phillips. It is designed around a balanced eating plan, strength training and a cardio program. I was inspired by the before and after pictures of the previous winners, and I was certainly motivated to start the program.

Two main sources motivated me. I asked myself: "What will happen if I take the 12-week Body-for-Life Challenge?" and "What will happen if I don't take the 12-week Body-for-Life Challenge?"

If I follow the program, I will lose weight, feel better about myself and also look better. If I don't take the challenge, I will continue to carry excess weight and have a poor self-image.

When I decided to take on the Body-for-Life Challenge, I didn't realize how hard it would be to stick to a program. It was a great program, but there were certain guidelines to follow, and I would only see results if I followed the plan. The exercise was easy. I loved to work out (still do!). The eating part was not so easy. I loved to eat! The Body-for-Life Challenge allowed for one cheat day of eating, which meant I could eat everything and anything in any amount. My cheat day was Sunday. In order to stay on track on the program, I had to listen to motivational tapes. Every day, I would look at the before and after pictures of previous contestants, because they inspired me to stay on course. It was great to have a "cheat day," and I anxiously looked forward to that day. However, during the week, it was so hard not to eat the foods I enjoyed; I felt deprived. Sunday seemed to take forever to arrive!

Even though it was a challenge to complete the 12-week program, I honored my self-promise and reached my goal of sticking with the plan. My success in the program was very dependent on listening to motivational CDs and inspirational messages.

I often reflect on the time I achieved my weight-loss goal and it helps to remind me that I can do whatever I set my mind to. This experience helped me to develop character and as a result, I can follow those same principles and apply them to whatever other goals I want to achieve.

Self-motivation: Without it nothing else works.
With it, nothing else matters.

– Richard B. Brooke

It's easy for us to lose our motivation. However, the only way to really lose motivation is to just give up. I don't believe you are like that; otherwise, you would not be reading this book about how you, too, can overcome challenges and obstacles in your life and achieve your goals and dreams.

If you focus on "can't," you will not have any energy or enthusiasm to go after your dreams. However, if you focus on "can," you will have energy and enthusiasm to burn! You will be motivated to succeed.

Inspiration versus Motivation — Notes

Here are six steps that are required in the process of motivation.

1. *Desire.* First, to be motivated you must have an intense, burning desire to get where or what you want.

2. *Decision.* You must make a conscious decision about what to aim for.

3. *Determination.* Climb mountains so that absolutely nothing will stop you. You need to be able to repeat the habits which are necessary to get there.

4. *Discipline.* It is critical to pay the price whether you like it or not. Motivation is strongest when it is the internalization of your goals and dreams—in other words, when you are headed on a clear path in your life's direction.

5. *Focus.* You need to stay focused and not become easily distracted by everyday life. Things will happen and you will have to attend to them, but don't let them throw you off so that you lose sight of your goals.

6. *Purpose.* Once you find your purpose, you *will* be motivated. Purpose comes from enthusiasm and is lit by our passions.

✦ ✦ ✦

✦   What distractions are taking your focus off of getting what you want?

✦   List some of these distractions.

How to handle the dream stealers: determination

*If I had to select one quality, one personal characteristic
that I regard as being most highly correlated with success,
whatever the field, I would pick the trait of persistence.
Determination. The will to endure to the end, to get
knocked down seventy times and get up off the floor
saying, "Here comes number seventy-one!"*

– Richard M. Devos

I was determined to succeed no matter what the challenge or obstacle. Yet, this can be extremely difficult when the people closest to you don't support your goals and dreams. I call these *dream stealers*. Dream stealers are the people who make you believe that you'll never reach your dreams. They're the people that encourage you to play it safe. For instance, to get a nice safe job and to marry the boy you went to high school with. Does this sound a lot like your parents? That's not surprising because family members are often the worst offenders when it comes to stealing your dreams.

I was criticized by my family for pursuing my degree program. Maybe it was out of concern. However, the way it came across, I did not feel like I was being supported in my endeavors. It's interesting to observe that nothing has changed in this respect and perhaps it was because change was uncomfortable or they didn't have any goals or dreams or were too scared to go after them. Whether I went on the 12-week Body-for-Life Challenge, changed jobs, started a business or learned new skills, I didn't feel I had family support. For years, I thought I had a problem because I loved to learn and experience new and different things, but over time, I realized that I thrived on challenge and change and wanted to experience all that I could. Their fears held them back.

You may even know of family or friends who have tried to hold you back from pursuing your goals and dreams. Perhaps they had fears of success, and because they had fear, they held themselves back from going after their own dreams. And as a result of giving up an opportunity to live their dreams, they can't stand to see you succeed where they failed.

There are countless times that I could tell you about where I didn't get the support that I wanted. Finally, one day I asked myself: "When are you going to stop looking for approval?" Sure, it would have been a nice bonus to have a cheering squad behind me every step of the way for all my achievements, but it really didn't matter. I learned to get up after being knocked down. I found the support I needed *inside me,* and it has only made me stronger. In fact, I believe I turned it into my success strategy. Instead of the word "no" debilitating me, I used it to empower me to achieve a whole new level of greatness I never dreamed possible. You can use this strategy as a life philosophy. Here's how Jesse Owens put it:

We all have dreams. But in order to make dreams come into reality, it takes an awful lot of determination, dedication, self-discipline, and effort.

As a result of my determination to go after my dreams, I've learned how to protect myself from being disappointed or hurt. I now keep my dreams to myself. I keep them safe, and I only tell people who share my vision and who understand and will support and encourage me. You may find that what I do to keep my dreams safe will help you as you move forward in pursuing your dreams.

How to Handle the Dream Stealers: Determination — Notes

Here's my success strategy on handling dream stealers:

1. I only share my dreams with the people who will be excited about what I want to accomplish with my life. This is important because you do not want to run the risk of dream stealers stealing your energy. You may find, like I did, family members do not understand and support and encourage your dreams. Find others who will. I talk about this book and my other projects with people who support and encourage me.

2. I will only share my successes but not my failures, because when I talk about my successes, it makes me feel good and gives me confidence. I never share my failures with the dream stealers because they take that as validation of their opinion that I would never succeed.

3. I plan my defense. If someone asks: "Why didn't you tell me that you were writing a book?" I tell them that I wanted to have it done before I told anyone because I knew it was a big goal, and I didn't want any negative input. I wanted to actually see if I could do it.

4. I remember that it is *my* dream. Not anyone else's. Everyone may have their ideas about how I should live my life and what I should do with my life. But—this is the best part—everyone gets to choose what they want to do with their own life. I may smile and thank them for their interest and their opinion, and I may even tell them what I learned from John Di Lemme, "I respect your opinion about my dream, but I respect my dream more than your opinion." Live your dreams on your own terms!

+ Write out the names of the people closest to you.

+ Can you share *all* your dreams with all of these people?

+ Write out the names of people you can share *all* your dreams with and feel safe.

HEY GREEN BAY PACKER!

*When you look in the mirror and hate what you see,
you need addictions to survive. If you don't like the
main character in your story, then everything and
everyone in it becomes a nightmare. But if you accept
yourself 100%, then you trust yourself. And whatever
you want to manifest in the world will happen.*

– Don Miguel Ruiz

Many women struggle with self-image and insecurity. Some women have based their self-worth around taking care of their family. Others base it on their looks, and they will go to extreme measures to try and measure up to what men or society says is acceptable. They've lost touch with their true identity because they look for others to tell them how they look or how they feel. And there are a lot of women out there who are insecure in their relationships. They don't feel as though they are good enough, and I believe that has everything to do with self-image and early mental conditioning.

I didn't know the Green Bay Packers were a football team, but it was my first nickname, given to me by some boys in my school. I was called Green Bay Packer because I looked quite bulky and big.

By the time I was 15 years old, my weight had skyrocketed and it was all stacked on my behind! That was probably the reason I was also nicknamed Freight Train. The boys would tease and mimic by walking with their butts stuck out … the way I looked and walked.

I hated the way I was putting on weight, and during a period of six months I had tried so many diets. You may have heard of the cabbage soup diet, the grapefruit diet and others … I was on the "All-You-Can-Eat" diet. It was so hard to diet, especially after a fresh batch of Mom's chocolate brownies came out of the oven!

I would try to starve myself, but then I would have sugar lows and I would try to eat everything and anything to feel good.

When I lived and worked on the farm, I only ate three meals, because I often only stopped working in the field for meals. I was always famished by the time I came in from the field. Of course, I overate then too, and it was a way to reward myself for my hard work.

I was on a roller-coaster ride and yo-yoing up a few pounds and down a few pounds. Hard as I tried, I couldn't seem to get a handle on controlling my weight gain and any attempts to losing the weight didn't seem to work. I just became more frustrated.

It's really no surprise that I did not feel good about myself, because I was now overweight, and I was continually teased and called names throughout high school. I worked very hard at school and tried so hard to be at the top of the class. I figured, if I was going to be fat, I was going to be smart too.

This was a way that I could compensate for my weight, and put the focus on being at the top of my class. I thought my self-image would improve if I excelled at my studies. Even though I did eventually achieve the highest standing upon high school graduation, it didn't make a difference in how I felt.

I felt that my weight was a big factor in my self-image and I tied it to my self-worth. I believed that if I was thin I would be happy, because I saw one of my sisters that way. She was fit, healthy and most importantly, happy. She was my best friend and I loved being around her because she was everything I wanted to be. And she never ever teased me. In some respect, I believe she was my saving grace, even when I was often down and out about my weight problem.

When women have abdicated their own identity to what others think and say, they tend to be very insecure in their relationships. They pick the wrong men for all the wrong reasons. They "settle" because they don't feel as though they are good enough to have a really terrific guy. I definitely settled for someone in my first marriage, and I know that the reasons I picked him had everything to do with my poor self-image at the time.

Our self-image is determined by how we think we compare to other people and also by what others think, as opposed to accepting ourselves and feeling good about who we are. For most of my life, I was influenced by what other people thought and over the years I developed a bad self-image. Because of this, I made decisions that resulted in bad choices which only made me feel worse about myself. But when I decided to take responsibility for my life, I developed courage and confidence and that really helped me change my life.

As a very young child, I was very skinny and I looked sickly. I was very pale. In fact, people who would visit us at our farm would say to my mom that it looked like they didn't love me, because I didn't look healthy compared to the other kids.

I also had many health challenges and one of them was suffering from chronic constipation. This might not seem like it could affect how I felt about myself until you think about how difficult this problem really is to confront by most people. It seemed the rest of my siblings were normal and I wasn't, or if they suffered from the same challenge I never knew because who talks about constipation?

I always was so troubled by my condition. I can remember as a young child feeling bad about myself. For many, many years I ignored my problem, hoping and praying every night that I would wake up and have a bowel movement. I was often sluggish, lethargic and seemed to be always sick. The worst part about the whole thing, though, was that it affected how I looked.

We're always conscious of our appearance, and because of my condition, I was always catching colds and with them came cold sores that would erupt over my face. I would pretend that I was normal, yet deep down my self-esteem was low and so was my self-image.

By the time I reached puberty at age 14, my skin color really didn't change a whole lot. I was still a bit pale, but what changed was I began gaining weight: a lot of it! And it didn't stop! I started packing on the pounds and I was no longer thin. I just loved to eat!

Getting fat is one of the worst problems a young girl has to face, but I couldn't stop eating. My mom was a phenomenal cook and because we lived on a grain and livestock farm, we lived off the land and she always prepared meals from scratch. My favorite was homemade bread, perogies and pies. Desserts were my best friend, my comforter, and I became the queen of junk food. If I was feeling down, I could always count on a Cuban Lunch chocolate bar to make me feel better!

As I reflect, I realize how my self-image led to my lack of self-confidence, which led me to make decisions that resulted in bad choices. But, just like I had a decision to make sitting in my wheelchair being laughed at by two old men, I needed to make one about all the physical problems I had.

Perhaps you can relate to one or more of my experiences. Maybe you feel you have failed and as a result your self-image and self-confidence have plummeted. Don't beat yourself up about it and don't think that you can't do anything about it. I hope you see that no matter what you have done or what choices you made, it doesn't mean your life is over. What I love is that today is a new day and it is a clean slate for you and me to enjoy. Oprah says, "Now that I know different, I do better." There is no sense beating ourselves up over mistakes of the past. There are no such things as mistakes, only lessons.

Instead, the way to take positive action about this issue is to acknowledge your mistakes or failures and move on. Look at what you did—the decisions that you made and the actions you took that got you into the undesirable condition. Say to yourself that you will succeed the next time. Never make the mistake of allowing your failures to overwhelm you or keep you down, because they will destroy your self-confidence.

Understand that our self-image is often dictated by our environment. We conform to other people's beliefs, and we are influenced by our parents too. They were our teachers. It's been said that 85% of families are dysfunctional and that environment can contribute to defining who we think we are.

There were things that I couldn't physically overcome easily —but, as an adult, I learned that bedwetting is a condition that plagues a small percentage of people and it can be remedied, rather than condemned or abused. Chronic constipation can be resolved by educating oneself about proper diet and nutritional supplementation, and Hepatitis B can be avoided by not sitting directly on public toilet seats and by using proper covers. As I grow older, I find that if I look at what happened I can learn from the situation and thus prevent it, or something like it, from happening again.

So now, when I make mistakes—and I still do, we all do!— I look at them as taking on a new challenge. I look for the positive in them and vow to do better next time. Life is a journey. Like good stories, we don't want them to end, but isn't it nice to know that we can control the outcome of each chapter!

Hey Green Bay Packer! — Notes

✦ How do you feel about yourself?

> Right now?
> Usually?

✦ Would you describe the way you feel about yourself *now* as a healthy self-image?

✦ Would you describe the way you usually feel about yourself as a healthy self-image?

✦ Would you like to change the way you feel about yourself?

6

You Don't Have to Get It Right

*You don't have to get it right,
just get it going!*

This is a great quote that I heard for the first time when I listened to a CD, "Your Greatness Held Hostage," a motivational message by Mike Litman.

I thought, "But how do I just get it going?" Here is how:

- Just start.
- Take small steps.
- Get going.
- Trust yourself.
- Believe in yourself.

Ask yourself: What is one thing I've been putting off that if I did today would help me or my business move forward? Can you do it within the next five hours? Of course you can.

When we were young and learned to color, our teacher would tell us to stay inside the lines. In order to be creative, we learned that it had to be done in a particular way, because that is what we were told. We were told to sit a certain way, talk a certain way and be a certain way. This led us to believe we couldn't do certain things unless we did them perfectly or according to someone else's standard. As a result, we became scared, in case we did something the wrong way, and so we allowed our fears of failing to paralyze us from doing something we wanted.

At an early age, I was a perfectionist; I set high standards for myself and expected the same of other people. Working with my dad, I was expected to do the job perfectly, because he held high standards. He didn't demand more of anyone else, though, than he did of himself, and I felt pressured to do well at everything. I carried on his values in my own life and they became a measure in anything that I set out to do. In some respect, these high standards groomed me for employment; I had two very demanding bosses when I worked in the administrative field and they were anal about having everything done to perfection. In other aspects of my life, it didn't serve me.

I was so conditioned to being a perfectionist that I would be quick to point out errors at a presentation or committee meeting. It annoyed me to find a typing mistake in a published book, and in any articles I read I would have a habit of circling the errors. It proved nothing more than I was a good proofreader. In their book, *How to Raise Your Manifestation Vibration: The Universal Secrets to Receiving Unlimited Success,* Jafree Ozwald and Margot Zaher talk about the mistakes and typos in their manual, how they were placed there for a reason and how we can explore those grammatical blunders as opportunities for personal growth. They suggest using each flaw in life, in yourself, in others and the text in the manual as a catalyst to awaken you, so you may refocus on the higher vibrations of forgiveness, laughter and surrender. I did a paradigm shift after I read that one short paragraph. It was very insightful, and since then I haven't even twitched when I found an error in anything I've read.

Now that I am continually developing my business, I think that it's important to always strive for excellence, but it doesn't necessarily have to be perfect. I realize that I will not and cannot do everything to perfection. It's more important that I "get it going!" When I keep this in mind it helps me to take action and it has also helped me to relax as I learn from my mistakes and focus on improving.

Mediocrity is a sin.
Don't do your bit; do your best.

– William F. Halsey, Jr.

The most important thing is to just get going—take action on your goals. Procrastination is the biggest thief, and the longer we procrastinate, the longer we delay our future. It's uncomfortable getting uncomfortable, but once you make a decision to take action toward your goals and dreams, you will feel empowered.

We all have a tendency to put things off for various reasons and believe me, it is very easy to delay doing things. Understanding why you procrastinate helps you to do something about it. For most people, procrastinating is a way to put off something you really don't want to do.

I didn't like to study, and I didn't like to have to spend a lot of time preparing for an exam. I felt I was more efficient and retained the materials if I crammed. I would find anything else to do aside from studying.

How often have you made yourself "busy" just because you're putting off doing something you're resisting? When you put off a task it can start to develop almost ogre-like proportions before you get round to doing it. The longer you leave it, the harder it becomes. Usually by that time, it's become urgent or critical rather than just important.

When you are putting off something, ask yourself: What is the benefit of procrastinating? What is the payoff from putting this thing off? It may be the easier route in the short-term but what is the long-term impact?

> *The greatest thief this world ever produced is procrastination and he is still at large.*
>
> – Henry Wheeler Shaw

I found that cramming for an exam was not the most strategic approach, especially when all of a sudden my son was sick for the day prior to it. Procrastination does have consequences for your business, health or emotional well-being.

If you leave it too long, the task gets to the point where it can no longer be ignored and demands your attention. Now you have to get it done—which somehow, you now find the time or inclination to do, so what was stopping you in the first place?

When the pain of not doing something becomes greater than the pain of doing it, resistance will magically disappear, and more often than not you will find that it wasn't as bad as you thought after all.

Procrastination is a dream destroyer. Mike Litman said: "It's like a big bomb exploding violently on our personal goals. The things we deeply cherish. After the explosion, all that's left is ... regrets."

What if you don't stop procrastinating and make a change? Does it frighten you to think that your health may further decline? Your debt will continue to increase? Your business will take a nose dive?

"The principle of concentration is the medium by which procrastination is overcome. The same principle is the foundation upon which both self-confidence and self-esteem are predicated." This is from Napoleon Hill.

Procrastination is a thief. Run from it ... *now*!

You Don't Have to Get It Right — Notes

Here are few things that I have found helpful to prevent procrastination.

1. *Break it down.* To help reduce procrastination, try breaking a larger task down into smaller tasks, so it doesn't seem quite so onerous. For instance, writing a book is a pretty big task, and it can be overwhelming. What I did was create an outline to get started, and then I created some topics within the outline.

2. *Quick bites.* The easiest way I have found to tackle many things is by spending just 5 or 10 minutes on a task. You'll increase your productivity when you give yourself a time limit and it's less daunting than needing to spend an hour or more on it and less excuse to procrastinate. When I started to write, I would set a time limit

of 15 minutes to write non-stop. This helped me focus and stick to the task, and by doing this several times throughout the day, I made progress.

3. *Just do it!* Putting something off like a phone call or an e-mail? Instead of saying to yourself, I'll do it in a minute, or I'll do it later, do it now. Just do it *now*, and get it out of the way. Then you can move on and stop worrying. I find this works really well. Catch yourself putting something off and just do it. It was difficult for me to even set 15 minutes aside to write if I was thinking about an errand I had to run. If I couldn't delegate the errand, I was far more productive when I just went and did it and then came back to my writing.

4. *If it's worth doing—do it now!* If it's not, then just let it go and stop worrying about it.

+ Break down one of your goals into small steps.

+ List the steps.

+ What is *one thing* you can do in the next five hours that will move you closer to your goal?

+ Set a time when you will finish that one thing.

WE ALL HAVE THE SAME AMOUNT OF TIME IN A DAY

Time = life,
Therefore, waste your time
And [you] waste your life,
or master your time and
[you] master your life.

– Alan Lakein

"There aren't enough hours in the day," I would often tell myself.

Have you heard yourself say this?

Let's face it. As women, we have a lot of responsibility and it is a challenge to fit it all in within a day. Lauren Hudson, motivational speaker, says women have to cram a 48-hour workload into a 24-hour day! We are employee, wife, mother, lover, friend, daughter, limo driver, housekeeper, chef, teacher, counselor, etc. The list goes on.

H. Jackson Brown had it right when he said: "Don't say you don't have enough time. You have exactly the same number of hours per day that were given to Helen Keller, Louis Pasteur, Michelangelo, Mother Teresa, Leonardo daVinci, Thomas Jefferson and Albert Einstein."

First of all, time cannot be managed; it flows. When you learn to lead and manage yourself to integrate all areas of your life, you will find it's not something you specifically need to do. Imagine that all those feelings of panic, procrastination and being in a hurry were not in your life. Feeling out of control comes when you have lost touch with what is important to you and you end up doing too much of what doesn't matter or doing nothing. In order for me to take a University degree, while being a full-time employee and mom, I had to be focused. My day started at 5:00 AM and often I wasn't in bed before midnight. It was a lot to fit in the day, and there were days when I felt like something had to give. At times I was so tired, but I felt the one thing that I was doing for myself was getting ahead by studying. The job, the kids and house were all things that I had to do and they were just part of life. I had to figure out a way to get everything done. I had to get organized and stay focused.

Each day, I would know what I needed to do to stay on track with my courses and the other duties fell in around that. It was very important that I spent time with my boys, so I rarely started studying before 8:00 PM. I trained myself not to need as much sleep, as I had to find some extra time in the day to study. I also liked to exercise, because I found that it gave me so much more energy, so I had to fit time in for exercise. For years now, I've made it a habit to get up at 5:00 AM so I can fit in my workout before I start my day. Then I had to get my kids up, feed and dress them and leave the house by 7:15 AM, drop them off at the baby-sitter and then drive for another 20 minutes to be at work by 8:00. I managed the schedule like clockwork and it was a full day!

Now that I have my own business and make my own schedule, I constantly need to implement time management and plan my days. I find when I do this, I accomplish more in less time. Someone said: "Failing to plan is planning to fail" (author unknown).

I read that by the time we reach age 60, we will have slept for 20 years or one-third of our life! (People sleep on average 8 hours a night.) The morning after I heard that, I bolted out of bed. I didn't want to waste too much time sleeping!

When you think about having 24 hours a day minus the 8 hours we sleep, it leaves us with 16 productive hours to accomplish things that need to be done at home and at work. Of these 16 hours, a lot of time is wasted due to distractions, interruptions and disorganization. How many times have you heard "I don't have time" or "There isn't enough time"? That simply is not true. We all have the same amount of time in a day which is 24 hours (1,440 minutes), and what we do with our time is our choice.

We All Have the Same Amount of Time in a Day — Notes

There are many things that are time wasters. I've listed the top six time wasters, and by avoiding them I've found that I am able to accomplish so much more.

1. *Television.* We average four hours a day watching television. If we live to be 72 it works out to 12 solid years wasted watching TV. Yikes! This doesn't include time spent on the Internet. Solution? Go on frequent television fasts, or better yet, eliminate it! Just try for a week and see how much you get accomplished.

2. *E-mailing back and forth.* E-mail becomes time-consuming when you consider how often we check it and how frequently we are involved in sending back and forth messages.

3. *Junk mail* of the traditional kind. Too much time is wasted opening and then trashing unwanted mail.

4. *Drop-in visits.* When you are in your office with the door open you are an open invitation to those with nothing better to do to drop in for a chat. When they do, they eat up a lot of your precious time. Solution? Keep your door closed. If you don't want to close your door arrange your desk in such a way that people passing by can't see you and they won't drop in for a visit.

5. *Reading every word of every document or e-mail that crosses your desk.* We are living in the age of information and it seems that much of it ends up on our desk each day demanding our attention. Learn how to scan it quickly and either discard it or place it in your "for further study" pile; otherwise, you will end up over-whelmed and stressed.

6. *Phone calls which are too long and too frequent.* Some people just won't get off the phone and let you get back to work. Solution? Let people know that it is a bad time and then give them a better time to call when you can spare a few minutes. Before they call back, intend to keep the conversation to the point and brief.

❄ ❄ ❄

+ Over the next week, write out the amount of time you spend watching TV.

+ Write out how much time you spend (1) reading, (2) writing and (3) answering e-mails that are not related to your goals.

+ Keep track of how much time you spend on the phone— or in other activities which are not related to your goals.

THE POWER OF INTENTION

Go for it now.
The future is promised to no one.

– Wayne Dyer

Some time ago, I read Dr. Wayne Dyer's book, *The Power of Intention*, which gave me a good understanding of how we can be, do and have anything, by just setting our mind on that particular thing.

A working definition for intention is "to have in mind a purpose or plan, to direct the mind, to aim." Lacking intention, we sometimes stray without meaning or direction. But with it, all the forces of the universe can align to make even the most impossible, possible.

This works for me almost 90% of the time. When I go to the store, I go with the intention of finding a parking spot nearby. When I do this, it almost always happens. I may have to drive around for a minute, but a spot almost always becomes open. I find this exercise entertaining, and it's more fun when my son is with me because I can teach him how powerful this is. I apply the power of intention daily now, and I find that when I do, the things that I want to happen, do!

When you set your mind to doing something, do it, and expect that it will get done. Let me ask you, have you ever gone to the grocery store for milk, and thought to yourself, there probably won't be any milk?

People set intentions on all kinds of dreams: to get married or have children, to get a job or make a career change, to write a book or lose weight. When you set an intention and then act on it to demonstrate your commitment, amazing things occur. Intention can also give us strength for dealing with tough times.

When my husband lost his job because the position was eliminated, it was devastating. And worse yet, people thought it was something he had done that caused it. A realtor from an agency we never did business with came to our house within the hour of my husband losing his job and assumed we were selling and he wanted to list our home. I couldn't believe it! My intention was to hold my head high and live through this process with dignity and grace.

It's often not easy, but this intention has helped me maintain composure, sanity, and on a good day, a sense of humor. Intention can be used for anything.

If you want to make changes, you can maximize the power of intention to increase the effectiveness of intention in your life by using the following as a guide. I have become conscious about my intentions since I applied these principles and it does work. The more attention is placed on intention—my experience is—the more magic shows up. I encourage this practice.

The Power of Intention — Notes

1. Be *clear* about your desires. Would you like to receive an extra $2,000 next month? Do you want to have more energy? Do you want to attract your ideal mate? Whatever your desire, intention can accelerate the results. The more *clarity* you have, the better.

2. Get *connected*. Realize that you are not separate from your desire. Imagine and experience yourself receiving your intention now. How does it feel? The more fully you associate with your intention, the better. Abraham-Hicks said, "Desire summons life force. If we must continue to be alive, we must continue to have new desire."

3. *Believe.* Your thoughts shape your reality. If you don't think "intention" can work, it probably won't. If you don't believe that you'll be able to attract your desire, you probably won't.

4. *Trust* the process. Once you've set an intention, it's time for trust and faith to set in. When you put a cake in the oven, you don't question that it will bake. You also don't have to understand how the dough is transformed into a dessert. Have faith in the process.

5. Be *unattached* to the outcome. Allow your desires to unfold in the perfect time and manner. When we are attached to a specific outcome, the energy becomes restricted and we cut off the natural flow of energy. It's also useful to not be attached to a timeline. Everything

unfolds in its perfect order. Oftentimes you will receive something *better* than what you imagined in your mind.

6. Be *open* to receiving. Often an intention may be blocked energetically by an underlying belief. Do you feel you are truly worthy and deserving of *receiving* your intention? Jacquelyn Aldana, author of *The 15-Minute Miracle Revealed*™, says that life cannot (and will not) bring you the objects of your desire until you are ready and willing to *accept* them.

+   Write out or record every detail (in great detail) about your desires.

+   Detach yourself from the outcome. If needed, pretend you are an observer viewing all the details as someone else is narrating all the details.

+   Take a deep breath. Believe you will attract your desire.

+   Be open to receiving. This might be more difficult than you thought!

7

Habits: Friend or Foe?

RIDDLE: WHO AM I?

I am your constant companion.
I am your greatest helper or your heaviest burden.
I will push you onward or drag you down to failure.
I am completely at your command.
Half the things you do, you might just as well turn over to me,
and I will be able to do them quickly and correctly.
I am easily managed; you must merely be firm with me.
Show me exactly how you want something done,
and after a few lessons I will do it automatically.
I am the servant of all great men.
And, alas, of all failures as well.
Those who are great, I have made great.
Those who are failures, I have made failures.
I am not a machine, though I work with all the precision
of a machine, plus the intelligence of a man.
You may run me for profit, or run me for ruin;
it makes no difference to me.

Take me, train me, be firm with me,
and I will put the world at your feet.
Be easy with me, and I will destroy you.
Who am I?
I am a HABIT.

– Author unknown

D id you know that habits are incredibly powerful tools for personal growth and success?

Think about the habits you have now and how they affect
virtually every aspect of your life. Your weight and health are determined by your eating habits. Your relationships with people are
determined by your social habits. Your success at work is determined by your work habits. You have sleeping habits that dictate
how well you sleep. You even have buying habits; just take a look
around your house and you will quickly see them. Our character,
health and virtually every aspect of our lives are determined by
our habits.

If you ask ten people on the street what the word habit means,
nine out of ten will tell you that a habit is a negative action that
people do over and over again, like smoking, or procrastinating
or eating too much. These are definitely bad habits. But habits can
be positive, too.

A positive habit is simply a habit that produces positive benefits, actions and attitudes you want to acquire and make a part
of your life. There is such great power in positive habits to effect
change, because habits, by their very nature, are automatic. After
a period of time they can become permanent. Some people have
suggested that you can make positive changes within 21 days.
Mark Gorman, author of *God's Plan for Prosperity*, suggests it

takes fives minutes to change a habit. The most important part of developing a habit, though, is to just decide to have a positive habit; for example: I no longer want to hold on to the past. Take one small step toward making changes. Pastor T.D. Jakes said, "You can't take the next step while still holding on to the first step."

We all have good habits that we want to form. I desperately wanted to change my body weight. I had to change my eating habits and eat five to six very small meals a day and drink a lot of water. I had to replace a bad habit of overeating and snacking with exercise and drinking more water. It was a good habit to stop watching as much TV and take up exercise more frequently. If I ever found myself opening the fridge when I was not supposed to be eating, I would say to myself, "Is this moving me closer to my goal or is it moving me farther away from my goal?" Making changes was not easy, but I had a strong desire for change and that meant making changes in my daily routine right away.

Habits: Friend or Foe? — Notes

These were some of the habits I used which might be useful to achieve your goals.

1. Have a positive mindset.

2. Set a goal to exercise every day for 30 minutes. Whatever your goal, set time aside to work toward your goal.

3. Eat only foods that are within the program guidelines. Each evening I would write out the menu for the following day. You can do this for making a list of the items you need to accomplish in a day.

4. Remember *why* I took on the Challenge. Knowing *why* you want to achieve your goal will keep you motivated.

5. Surround myself with people who will support me. This is so critical to your success. Delete negative associations and seek out coaches and mentors who will help you succeed.

6. *Expect* to succeed—that is key!

✦ Write out in a list 7 to 9 of your habits.

✦ Are there some you want to change?

✦ Circle those habits you want to change.

VALUE OF HARD WORK

Working hard overcomes a whole lot of obstacles.
You can have unbelievable intelligence, you can
have connections, and you can have opportunities
fall out of the sky. But in the end, hard work is the
true, enduring characteristic of successful people.

– Marsha Evans

Big success is built on a series of small successes, and it is possible for anyone to do anything by capitalizing on their strengths and potential, rather than dwelling on their limitations and what they can't do. Women often feel that they have no place to contribute outside of their home or jobs because they feel they have limited skills. This is usually not the case, and the first step to becoming empowered is to draw from your experience, skills and talents that helped you as you grew up and even used in raising your children, managing your home or working on a job. For most of my life I discounted my abilities and really never put any value on the skills I learned while growing up. Once

I became much older, I started appreciating the skills I developed throughout my life and how I am now able to draw from those experiences.

Many of my skills were developed as a child while learning the value of hard work. I did not appreciate that lesson I learned through this until a quite a few years later; in fact, I rather resented having to work almost every day on the farm. Today, though, I'm grateful for being taught a good work ethic as this is what has helped me to have the discipline, determination and persistence to pursue my goals and dreams.

Beginning when I was eight years old, I helped on the farm. Being the second oldest child, I was expected to help. Even though I was a child, my dad appreciated the help and didn't expect my labor for free. He paid me 10 cents an hour, and he gave me a book to track my hours and always made sure he paid me. I really liked tracking my hours!

There were many days it was blistering hot and we would stay out in the field for hours and hours. We didn't wear sunscreen either—I'm not sure if it even existed! There also weren't any "rest" periods. On the weekends, for example, we learned to work hard until Dad said it was time for lunch, and then after lunch we would return to the field and work until dinner or sometimes until it was dark or when he was satisfied with the efforts for the day.

On days when we weren't working on the land, we would have to just follow Dad around the yard while he worked on machinery, just in case he needed us to run and get something for him. By the age of 13, I learned how to hook up machinery to the hydraulics and was driving the tractor and implements on the highway, as our sections of land were located miles apart. I was also skilled at driving the combine at harvest. There were times when we were harvesting till 1:00 or 2:00 AM, as it was critical to finish taking off the crop before a rain moved in. It was always amazing to be working late at night. I would watch the stars, and I would always look for the Big Dipper and the Little Dipper. Harvest time was my favorite time on the farm, especially when it was a bumper crop.

There was always something to do on the farm, except on rainy days. I sure welcomed those days, because it meant a day off from working on the land! Even today, I absolutely love a rainy day; I find them so relaxing.

By the time I was about 15 years old I had earned almost $1,600. This was a lot of money "back in the day"! I saved my money and loved to watch it grow. I was very proud of myself for that.

Right after high school graduation I started looking for a job. My parents and siblings were all going to visit relatives in another province for two weeks, and while I looked for employment I was also to look after the farm while everyone was away.

I started my first full-time job at the plywood mill at age 17, and it was hard work to be standing on cement flooring for eight hours, but I got paid extremely well at $12.97/hour. I pulled veneer off the dryers and it was a very demanding job—the machines spilled it off and if you didn't sort it quickly, all the wood would be piling up. It was the first experience in working with other people and I learned quickly that not everyone had the same work ethic.

Hard work spotlights the character of people:
some turn up their sleeves, some turn up
their noses, and some don't turn up at all.

– Sam Ewing

I gained valuable work and life skills like punctuality, team-work, working with all kinds of other people, maintaining the quality level and demonstrating initiative on the job. The wage was phenomenal and I enjoyed the people for the most part. I saved all my money to pay for my clerical assistant program. I learned (from my dad) that a person should not buy anything they couldn't pay for in cash. I worked hard to earn the money and I got great satisfaction as a result—I could make my decisions and support them financially.

While my early life was filled with much self-doubt, and while I certainly didn't always enjoy working on my family's farm, it taught me two invaluable life skills. I learned how to work hard and, more important, to stay committed until the job is done. Even when I was struggling through my failing marriage and then dealing with life as a single mom, I knew that as long as I knew how to work hard I could earn a living. I could always take care of myself. My little success of driving the tractor when I was eight years old gave me more confidence to think I had the potential to learn how to take on more responsibility on the farm. I learned how to earn money by working hard.

You, too, have learned many skills as a child, teenager and young adult, and you can transfer all those things into anything you want to be, do and have … *now*! Eliminate self-doubt and become empowered and inspired by what you have accomplished in your life. Use your accomplishments to give you the wind beneath your wings to become all that you were meant to be.

Value of Hard Work — Notes

✦ Now that you have thought about your skills, make a list of as many of your skills as you can.

Can't think of any? Contact me at 701-205-4077, or e-mail Julie@expectsuccessbeunstoppable.com.

Is your list less than 20? If it is, keep going.

✦ Which are your best skills? Which of these do you think also reflect your strengths and talents?

✦ Can any of your skills be used to reach your goals?

WATCH YOUR WORDS

We cannot always control our thoughts,
but we can control our words, and
repetition impresses the subconscious
and we are then master of the situation.

– Florence Scovel Shinn

As I write my book I am constantly monitoring my thoughts. This is the biggest project I've ever done, and because it is my personal story, it's so easy to question, "Who would find my story of interest?" and "This is just way too hard."

Just like you need an oil filter for your car, a coffee filter for your coffeemaker and virus software to protect your computer, so too you need a language filter. This language filter is to protect you from any negative talk to yourself or from anyone else.

The words that you say to yourself, in your mind and out loud, will have an impact on how you are feeling.

Here are some words that describe negative emotions; do you use any of them? Write down some more of the common phrases that you use.

+ "I'm feeling tired"
+ "I'm stupid"
+ "I'm angry"
+ "I'm livid"
+ "I'm overwhelmed"
+ "I'm feeling insecure"
+ "I'm depressed"

The intensity of those negative sayings will have an effect on how you feel and whether you feel confident or not.

Just imagine that instead of saying to yourself: "I'm really nervous," you said: "I'm really excited." Do you think it would make you feel better? Words you use are indicative of your state of mind and truly create your reality. Even when joking, you betray your inner feelings with your word choices.

The words you use can have an impact on your business and your career. If you use the words "try" or "hope" (as in "I hope to do ...") you don't have the confidence that you will be successful. Tentative language is for tentative people.

How often have you heard: "I'll try?" People who are always "trying" usually aren't succeeding; they wear themselves out, but never quite make it. Trying is failing.

> *The state of your life is nothing more than*
> *a reflection of your state of mind.*
>
> – Dr. Wayne W. Dyer

Word choice is just that: choice. Listen to your language. What does it say about you? Does it reflect who you think you are or want to be? Changing your language can literally change your life. It won't happen suddenly. Pay attention. Watch your language. Make different word choices and you'll move your life in a new direction.

We are all too familiar with attitudes of a lot of employees, and many companies, who walk around saying "we can't" do something or "it's too hard" or "we don't have enough" or "it's not working" or "I just knew (whatever bad thing) was going to or is going to happen." It's frustrating to hear those words when you are expecting quality customer service.

Pastor Rob Yanok tells a story about the customer service he receives when he visits the Ritz-Carlton. All the employees are trained to say "I can do that" each and every time they are asked for assistance. Even if they can't do whatever it is, they never say they can't. The employees only respond positively.

Change your speaking right away. Look at the *big* picture. Here are some important insights shared by Frank Outlaw, Deepak Chopra, Wayne Dyer and others, about the whole process of what happens when you speak—starting with your thoughts.

- ✦ Watch your thoughts because they become words.
- ✦ Watch your words, they become actions.
- ✦ Watch your actions, they become your habits.
- ✦ Watch your habits, they become your character.
- ✦ Watch your character, for it becomes your destiny.

You can literally change your entire life by simply changing what you think and what you say. Your words are very powerful. They tend to follow your thoughts. Your words can work for you or against you. The choice is yours.

Watch Your Words — Notes

Here is an exercise to help you watch your words.

1. *Monitor your self-talk.* Today, practice saying very little. Do *not* react verbally to any news until you can speak positively (say something positive) in every situation.

2. *Use positive, concrete language.* A good way to really get a handle on how you speak is to get a tape recorder and walk around with it for a few days. Record everything you say and play it back at the end of the day. You'll be shocked—even while knowing you were being taped— what kind of negative, self-defeating and critical words you use in a day.

3. *Maintain perspective.* With enough repetition, habits become sticky and lead to creating patterns we integrate into our lives more automatically. It is inevitable that old habits of using negative words will surface, but now that you are aware, you can stop that "stink'n think'n" and change to using positive words.

+ Get a tape recorder and walk around with it for a few days. Record everything you say and play it back at the end of the day.

+ How many negative, self-defeating and critical words did you use in a day?

+ This can be very surprising!

You become what you think about

An affirmation is a positive state of [positive] belief, and if we can become one-tenth as good at positive self-talk as we are at the negative self-talk, we will notice an enormous change.

– Julia Cameron

An affirmation is a statement that you make to yourself. Everyone uses them intentionally or unintentionally. You wake up in the morning, jump out of bed and exclaim "I feel great! It is going to be an amazing day!" These are positive affirmations. On the other hand, if you drag yourself out of bed in the morning and whimper, "I feel terrible, how am I going to make it through the day?" these are negative affirmations. Both statements help to maintain the emotional state you are in.

Our self-talk, the things we say to ourselves, is very important because it directly affects our conscious and subconscious mind. We listen to everything we say to ourselves.

It is so important to use affirmations daily and often. I am applying and using affirmations as I write this book. I find fear and doubt perched on my shoulder, and I have to use affirmations to flick those two imposters off my shoulder! On the other side a negative voice whispers negative thoughts, attempting to break my spirits, my energy and my enthusiasm. The best way to get rid of these doubter guys is to flick them off your shoulder by saying affirmations.

It's the repetition of affirmations that leads to belief. And once that belief becomes a deep conviction, things begin to happen.

Your affirmations can include how you would like to feel: "I am energetic," I feel wonderful," or "I feel safe." Your affirmations can include how you would like your life to be: "I am a prosperous person," "I attract positive people into my life," "I lose weight easily," or "I solve problems easily." Another way to develop affirmations is to use them to counter your negative self-talk. When you catch yourself saying something negative to yourself, develop an affirmation that counteracts the negative thought and start using it until you feel differently about yourself.

Let's say you are working on a project. The project doesn't have to be a work project, it can be an interpersonal problem or just some personal problem you are trying to solve. You can't seem to figure out what to do or you run into a snag of some sort. All of a sudden your confidence sags and you catch yourself thinking "I can't do this. I bit off more than I can chew or do. I'm just not smart enough."

All this negative thinking, if allowed to persist, will guarantee failure. Instead, make up some affirmations to counter this thinking. For example, you might use "I feel confident. I am a success. I do things now and I think clearly." Repeat each affirmation five times three or four times during the day until you feel better about yourself and about completing the project.

Used correctly, affirmations for personal growth and self-improvement can help relieve your depression, anxiety, fear and anger. They can help you lose weight as well as quit smoking. Affirmations will help you build your self-confidence, self-esteem and assertiveness, and they are an excellent tool for stress management.

Some examples of affirmation might be:

+ "I earn X amount of money" (use your Big Dream).
+ "I weigh 150 pounds."
+ "I eat only healthy foods."
+ "I am on the road to financial responsibility."

Studies have concluded that every person in the world has ongoing dialog or self-talk of about 50,000 thoughts a day. That's two thoughts each second! It's important to use all these thoughts in a positive way. Keep the positive thoughts in and the negative thoughts out of your mind.

You become what you think about.

– Earl Nightingale

Using affirmations daily has helped me accomplish my goal of writing my book. Often I would have doubts about my ability to write my book and I would flick "the doubter man" off my shoulder by affirming: "I am so happy *now* that I am a published author." The more I said it the more I believed it, and it really motivated me to keep writing.

You Become What You Think About — Notes

Here are some tips on creating and using affirmations.

1. *Begin with "I."* The most important aspect of an affirmation is that you need to make it personal and it needs to start with "I." Some examples: I am kind. I am helpful. I smile at people I see. I am punctual. I am hard-working.

2. *Use present tense* (i.e. "I am"). Affirmations should be in the present tense. Keep the statement in the moment. By keeping it in the present tense, your subconscious can go to work on it immediately.

3. *Be concise.* Affirmations should be in short, powerful sentences. Your subconscious mind needs a clear message, so stay away from long drawn-out sentences. Clarity is power.

4. *Repeat, repeat, repeat.* You need to repeat your affirmations as often as possible. Ideally you want to do this twice a day, once when you get up in the morning and then before you go to bed at night. When you do this before going to bed, you give your subconscious plenty of time to work on this key rewiring of your thought process. Take about 45 to 60 seconds for each affirmation. Keep repeating them with feeling. The more feeling you put into your affirmations, the sooner you're going to get results.

8

Close Your Eyes
and Imagine

*Picture yourself vividly as winning and that
alone will contribute immeasurably to success.
Great living starts with a picture, held in your
imagination, of what you would like to do or be.*

– Author unknown

Wallace D. Wattles in his book, *The Science of Getting Rich*, says that we must form a clear and definite mental picture of what we want, because we cannot transmit an idea unless we have it ourselves. "That clear mental picture you must have continually in your mind, and you must keep your face toward it all the time. You must no more lose sight of it than the steersman loses sight of the compass."

So what exactly is visualization? It is a technique of using your conscious mind to tell your subconscious mind all of your desires. Your mind really does work on two different levels. Using visualization will help you get both parts of your mind in alignment. The conscious mind is the logical, thinking mind that you are aware of and use every day. The conscious mind is under your direct control. You control your thoughts. Your thoughts influence your feelings, what actions you take and the results you get. Most people focus their attention on the conscious mind when trying to achieve their goals. They make plans, they employ positive thinking, and they still fail. Using only your conscious mind will get you nowhere fast. You have to use your subconscious mind as well.

Visualization is one of the most important things you can do to reach your goals and dreams. Performing daily visualization exercises has helped me achieve several life goals.

There is a very simple key to changing your dreams into realities. A lot of people miss this key. That is why some of them never reach their goals. We have been taught to set goals, put them in writing, make a solid plan, but none of these things are enough. If they were, we would all have everything we have ever dreamed of by now. Here is the missing link: *visualization*, which is to hold a picture in your mind and imagine the thing you want. This one thing is a powerful success tool.

For years I pictured myself at my convocation: I would be wearing my gown and graduation cap and I would be walking on the stage to receive my degree. It would be a most memorable event.

In fact, it was what I thought of especially when it seemed that I was making slow progress toward its completion. When I had failed one of my courses, linear algebra, it delayed my completion of the program and I really needed to tap into visualization: me receiving my degree.

When I ran in a triathlon, I pictured the finish line. It was a cold, rainy day and I had never competed in a triathlon. I loved a challenge, and I just had to enter to see if I could do it. I wanted to do it at least once, just to see if I could. I wanted to be able to say, "I went in a triathlon." The wind was especially strong and it was a challenge biking and running. All I kept picturing was the finish line. It worked.

The Body-for-Life Challenge really tested my ability to hold the picture of what I wanted to achieve. Early in the week I had a clear mental picture of my slim and toned body, but towards the end of the week the picture was a little foggy, because I was craving my favorite foods and I wasn't allowed anything except on my free day: my cheat day! I sure was anxious for Sunday, my cheat day! I managed to stay on track by continually refocusing on my slim, toned body mental picture, and it really helped me to meet my goal of successfully completing the Body-for-Life Challenge.

Seeing your picture (of what you want) is a powerful tool for building self-confidence. With a picture, you see in your mind's eye the accomplishment or goal that you want to achieve. By picturing each step in vivid detail, you change your perception of your capabilities by positively creating the reality you want in your mind. I pictured receiving my University degree, my triathlon medal and my Body-for-Life Challenge award.

Visualization can be a powerful key for anyone to achieve success. This can be in any area in our life, whether it is success in business, overcoming health issues or achieving success in sporting ventures.

Life does not consist mainly, or even largely, of facts and happenings. It consists mainly of the stream of thought that is forever flowing through one's head.

– Mark Twain

Visualization is a technique that has been used by successful athletes, actors, politicians and business people. It is a technique that can make the difference between success and failure. This technique may be used for both physically and mentally challenging goals.

Arnold Schwarzenegger, now the Governor of California, won the Mr. Universe title five times and he attributes his success to a great extent to using visualization to achieve that. He refers to the time before he won his first tournament. The title was already his. He had seen himself winning it so many times in his mind he had no doubt he would win it.

He makes the same claim about being a successful actor. He wasn't the greatest of actors but that did not stop him from being successful and earning big money.

Visualization is nothing more than using your imagination. It is a matter of creating in your mind what you want to be, do or have. It is like making a movie in your mind and you are the director. You have complete control.

If you watched *The Secret*, you may recall the man who survived the plane crash. He had multiple injuries and it was amazing he lived to talk about it. The doctors said he would never walk again, but he believed that he would walk again and he marked down the date that he would walk out of the hospital.

At this time, the only thing he was able to use was his mind. He could only blink his eyes and that is how he communicated to the nurses. They wrote out what he "blinked." And, he was able to use his mind. The doctors said he would never recover from his injuries, but he was not prepared to accept that and he vowed to himself he would walk out of the hospital, unaided, by Christmas. The crash was in March.

So while he lay there all that time he made use of his mind by using visualization. He astounded everyone with his recovery and he eventually walked out of the hospital, unaided, before Christmas as he had visualized and imagined that he would. He was determined to do this and he did!

(NOTE: Some people see a picture when they visualize a goal they want to achieve, others imagine reaching the goal. Both techniques work for visualizing. Editor)

Close Your Eyes and Imagine — Notes

Each and every one of us is capable of imagining or picturing. No special training is required. The results will amaze you. Here is how you can begin imagining/picturing.

Visualization is simply using your imagination. You create a scenario in your mind and imagine yourself as part of it. Even though the pictures may not be seen, they are still there, and most people can "feel" that picture is there. With practice, the more likely you are to start seeing those pictures more clearly. The key thing to realize about your mind is that it doesn't think in words. Your mind actually uses visual imagery to communicate or think.

1. Try this for at least 5 minutes at first; later you can do longer stretches of time. Sit down comfortably and relax. It helps to first concentrate on your breathing. The breathing is directly connected with the mind. Most people prefer to picture or imagine with closed eyes, but some prefer to do this process with open eyes.

2. Start by thinking about the goal you want to achieve.

3. Use your imagination and paint a picture of your life as if you have already achieved your goal. Get into the situation as much as you can. Include your emotions in the picture.

4. Enjoy your success. See your goal and your perfect life.

5. See yourself living a life full of love, bliss and abundance.

WRITE OUT YOUR GOALS

Almost every book on personal success and achievement outlines the importance of setting goals. You simply cannot go somewhere if you do not know where you want to go.

Og Mandino said it so clearly when he spoke these words: "The victory of success is half won when one gains the habit of setting goals and achieving them. Even the most tedious chore will become endurable as you parade through each day convinced that every task, no matter how menial or boring, brings you closer to achieving your dreams."

With goals we create the future in advance. With goals we literally create our destiny. We all have goals whether we know it or not. Some people's goals are to pay their bills or just make it through the day. The problem is that most people just have lousy goals. Lousy goals create a lousy life. Realize that no matter what your goals are, they are affecting your life every day you live it. We need goals that inspire us. With strong and compelling goals, we are driven to grow and expand and develop ourselves towards what we want from and for our lives. Compelling goals have the power to move us. Goals can transform our lives.

A study was done in 1953 at Yale University where they interviewed the graduating class just before they left school. They were asked among other things how many of them had a clearly defined set of goals with a written plan for its attainment. Only 3% had a clear plan for their lives with a specific set of goals. In 1973, 20 years later, they went back to interview the surviving class members of 1953 and they found that the 3% who had a set of written down goals seemed more happy, more well adjusted and more excited about their lives. The one very measurable thing was that the 3% who wrote down their goals were worth more financially than the other 97% combined.

Think of goals as drawing a map. If you know where you are and where you want to go, even if you do get lost you will find your ultimate destination, or your destiny. Set your goals way beyond your present abilities and position in life. Describe your ideal life without any inhibitions. You have got to get goals that are big enough to drive you—to excite you and thus drive you forward to where you want to be instead of just settling for whatever shows up in your life.

> *Goals are not only absolutely necessary to motivate us.*
> *They are essential to really keep us alive.*
>
> – Robert H. Schuller

We need to set goals in every area of our life. I have one-, three- and five-year goals in the areas of emotional, spiritual, physical, financial and relationships, as well as tangible or material goals. I set these short-, medium- and long-term goals at the beginning of the year and it felt amazing to see them written down. Going through the action of writing down my goals helped me to crystallize what I wanted to achieve. These goals have helped keep me on track toward my short-, medium- and long-term goals: the "grand plan" or vision for my life. It's important to reevaluate your progress from time to time, too, because doing this keeps you on track to see how you are progressing towards the "big picture." I find it extremely satisfying looking back and ticking off the goals I have achieved.

Pursuing our goals is important, for they have the power to move us. More importantly, though, we need to realize that at the end of our lives it is not the things we accumulated that will matter. What will matter is who we became as a person. This is the key. As you go through the process of making changes and moving toward your goal, you will be amazed at what you've learned along the way. I cannot emphasize this enough to you. I have learned and grown in so many ways, and even though I've accomplished some of my goals, I've more enjoyed the journey toward my goals because of the person I have become. Accomplishing my goals has given me the confidence to pursue bigger goals, goals that I never dreamed about before.

It's important to realize that we are not really after any "thing" in life but rather the way we think it will make us feel. You don't want more money, but you do want the way it will make you feel: that feeling of freedom, that sense of security, having the time to do what you want to do. Using these feelings we are striving for can help us define the goals we want for our life. It is critically important to know why you want something.

And, according to Robert Conklin, if you make the unconditional commitment to reach your most important goals, if the strength of your decision is sufficient, you will find the way and the power to achieve your goals.

Set your goals, regardless of previous "failures." Start fresh and do it properly. Come from a place of faith and believe, and watch your life soar to greater heights of happiness and fulfillment. Above all, enjoy life for it is a gift and live it with passion. It is all out there. The only thing that is required of you is to go and get it and realize that step one is to have a strong enough goal.

Whenever you make a mistake or get knocked down by life, don't look back at it too long. Mistakes are life's way of teaching you. Your capacity for occasional blunders is inseparable from your capacity to reach your goals. No one wins them all, and your failures, when they happen, are just part of your growth. Shake off your blunders. How will you know your limits without an occasional failure?

Never quit. Your turn will come.

– Og Mandino

The biggest reason for wanting to achieve my goal of obtaining my degree was to pursue other employment opportunities. I wanted to work at the college as an instructor. The only way I would be considered as a potential candidate was if I had a degree. I wanted the job at the college because it would allow me flexibility around my sons' activities, and I could pick them up for lunch; I would see them more. I would also have the summers off when they were off school. There wasn't a price tag big enough for me not to finish my degree. I was highly motivated to outline my goals in order to achieve them.

Whatever your goal, big or small, decide today that you are going to go after yours. Once you accomplish one goal it will empower you to go after bigger goals. Goals are the first step in a positive plan of action, and every journey starts with a small first step.

There are many benefits of setting goals, including:

+ Improves our self-confidence
+ Increases our motivation to achieve the most out of life
+ Able to achieve more in our lifetime
+ Helps to eliminate attitudes that hold us back and cause unhappiness
+ Improves our overall performance in life
+ Increases our pride and satisfaction in our achievements
+ Able to concentrate and focus better
+ We are happier and more satisfied with life
+ We suffer less from stress and anxiety
+ We perform better in all areas of life

In order to effectively achieve your goals in a timely manner, a helpful technique to consider is setting SMART goals.

The concept of SMART goals (specific, measurable, attainable, realistic and timely) is based upon specific steps used to encourage one to reach their potential beyond what they believe is attainable. One of the most important aspects of SMART goals is to set a deadline, which helps keep individuals moving towards accomplishing their dreams. Without a deadline, goals face the threat of staying stagnant, but when setting a targeted date for success, motivation becomes stronger.

Write Out Your Goals — Notes

Establishing SMART goals means that you approach their objective in a [S]pecific, [M]easurable, [A]ttainable, [R]ealistic and [T]imely manner.

Follow this SMART technique for writing out your goals.

1. *Specific.* Goals should be straightforward and tangible, and emphasize what you want to happen. My goal was to finish a Bachelor of Administration degree.

2. *Measurable.* Identify criteria for measuring progress toward the attainment of each goal you set. I set a goal to finish a course every two months.

3. *Attainable.* When you identify goals that are important to you, you begin to figure out ways to accomplish them. You develop the attitudes, abilities, skills and financial capacity to reach them. I developed the attitude of staying focused and being committed to studying at least three hours on a weekday.

4. *Realistic.* Your goals must be realistic. Keep all your goals within the realm of the possible. When I set my goal to finish a degree program, it was a big goal; in fact, at the time I really had no idea how I would achieve it. I'm sure glad I didn't worry about the how, and just focused on *why* I wanted to achieve my goal.

5. *Timely.* It is very important to put some sort of deadline on your goals. I set a deadline to finish my degree program, but at the time that I set it, I didn't anticipate having

another baby. The important thing to remember is that even though you miss your deadline, don't be discouraged. Someone said: "If you aim for the moon and hit the stars, it's okay." It is more important that you accomplish your goal.

THE LAW OF GRATITUDE

*The expression of gratitude is a powerful force that
generates even more of what we have already received.*

– Deepak Chopra

When I was a young child, I remember my mom waking us
up after we had gone to bed because my dad wasn't home.
He was off in the fields and she wanted to go and see if he
was okay. We all got dressed and headed down our "yellow" road
to where my dad was working. I wore my rubber boots (first thing
I grabbed to put on) and the tiny pebbles on the road hurt my feet
through my boots. It was pitch-black dark and I was so scared.

We all—Mom and my sisters and me—walked for about 30
minutes before Mom spotted my dad driving the tractor home.
Then we all turned around and walked back home. I was so thankful and grateful that my dad was okay and I was so grateful to crawl
back into my warm cozy bed. It was the first time I remember
feeling the feeling of gratitude; I didn't know exactly what gratitude was. I just remember how happy I felt inside. To this day, I
go to sleep with a thankful and grateful heart and a smile on my

face as I close my eyes. Each morning I wake up with a smile and thank God for another day, and I look forward to it with great expectation.

To have an attitude which is positive and enthusiastic will carry a person far in this world. It will affect the people around you. The attitude of a person will shape their outer world, whether they choose their attitude to be positive or negative. What I've found to be so helpful in keeping my attitude positive is reminding myself to be present in the moment of gratitude.

If you have an attitude of gratitude and give blessing to the people and world around you, you can dramatically draw more good into your life. Gratitude fulfills the law of multiplication. Whatever you genuinely feel grateful for, you multiply in your life.

Think about it. If you gave a gift to another and that person felt genuinely grateful for the gift, you'd want to give that person another gift, just so you could experience those wonderful feelings of appreciation and perhaps see a glow in another person's eyes, or feel really good about yourself for being able to do a good deed.

Well, the universe, or life in general, works exactly the same way. As you feel a deep sense of gratitude, you begin to release that wonderful vibration that draws into your life countless blessings.

We don't live in a universe of random chance or luck. We live in a universe that works by laws—predictable, repeatable, understandable laws.

The best book on these laws is the one written by Wallace Wattles, *The Science of Getting Rich*. He wrote: "There is a law of gratitude, and if you are to get the results you seek, it is absolutely necessary that you should observe this law."

Now, what is this law of gratitude and how does it work? Wattles tells us that it is an application of the law of cause and effect: "The law of gratitude is the natural principle that action and reaction are always equal and in opposite directions."

Here is what he means. We know that everything we put attention and emotional energy on, good or bad, will eventually show up in our lives. The universe and our subconscious mind don't know good from bad, and they treat fear and enthusiasm exactly the same. If we're putting energy on it, we're placing an order for it. It's important, then, to be putting positive energy on what we want, not negative energy (fear or worry) on what we don't want.

> *This is a great truth. The universe in which we live*
> *is strangely and wonderfully accommodating.*
>
> – Eric Butterworth

Gratitude is so important because it is a very high-energy positive vibration of thought. It is powerfully attractive! Wallace Wattles says it connects us with the Source. "You cannot exercise much power without gratitude because it is gratitude that keeps you connected with power. The creative power within us makes us into the image of that to which we give our attention. The grateful mind is constantly fixed upon the best; therefore, it will receive the best."

Do you see what Wattles is saying? If we are grateful about everything, we are focusing on what we want. It's a way of making sure we are putting the highest possible positive energy on our desires and withholding energy from the doubts and fears that we don't want.

This is the reason that almost everyone who teaches about goals insists that you see your goal as "already accomplished," and that you be grateful for it—*now*! It's a powerful way to be sure you're putting strong energy on the goal—using gratitude.

*People who can sincerely be thankful for things
which they own only in imagination have real
faith. They will get rich; they will cause the
creation of whatever they want.*

– Wallace Wattles

When you are grateful you will attract more things to be grateful for, and when you are grateful you are truly rich. Sir John Templeton, a very wealthy man, said it best: "When you are grateful for all the things in your life, you will have more things in your life to be grateful for." When you are grateful, you are open to receiving. Your vibrations are high. You are able to accept good things.

In order for me to be more aware and expressive of gratitude, I did the following exercises, which you may find helpful.

✦   Write down all the things you are grateful for that you already have in your life. Include all things in this gratitude, because it has all led you to this point where you will begin to consciously attract success.

✦   Make a collage or picture of everything you are grateful for. This is a very powerful way of expressing and reinforcing your gratitude because it takes time, energy and focus.

✦   Bring gratitude to as many moments as possible during your day, even the smallest things. In her book, *The 15-Minute Miracle Revealed*™, Jacquelyn Aldana tells us to set an intention to find ways to live every moment of our life in a state of profound gratitude and appreciation.

Doing these things to align yourself with gratitude is a very powerful spiritual practice which can change your life when done consistently. You can reprogram your mind by using gratitude to replace any thought of lack, resentment, disappointment, frustration or anger. Whenever a negative thought arises, replace it with gratitude. For example, if the thought arises, "He shouldn't have done that to me," it can be replaced with, "I'm grateful I have the strength and understanding to deal with this." In doing this, you move from victimization to peace, personal power and acceptance.

Whatever you put your attention on becomes stronger, so if you put your attention on what you are not grateful for, then feelings of lack, resentment, anger, disappointment and frustration will grow. On the other hand, if you give your attention to what you are grateful for, then the feeling of gratitude grows along with other positive feelings: joy, peace, contentment, acceptance and happiness.

Although it may not be possible to be grateful for having had a particular experience, we can learn to focus on being grateful for the growth or other positive things that came from it. No experience is without benefit. These benefits may be difficult to see when we are in the midst of a particular tragedy, but as time passes, it becomes easier. Ask yourself: How did that experience serve me? What was good about it? How have I grown as a result of it? The more you can focus on how something served you, the easier it will be to forgive, let go and move on. I believe we cannot truly help someone if we have not been in the situation; our experiences are there to help serve other people.

The use of gratitude on a daily basis in your life and in your affirmation practice is essential. So say "thank you" for those things that are here and for those things that have not yet manifested in your experience and you will find your affirmations practice yielding the results you want more quickly.

Success is not something that just "happens" to you. Success is something you either attract or repel. Think about what it is that you want and enjoy it like it is here already, and you are sure to attract success!

So how do you stay grateful in situations when you experience things that are not what you want or expected? In his book, *The Astonishing Power of Gratitude*, Wes Hopper offers five suggestions that will assist you in staying in a grateful mindset when facing challenges.

1. *The universe is friendly.* We know that the universe is moving us forward in an upward expansion of greatness. So everything that comes into our lives is there for us to learn from and grow into a greater person. Having this knowledge allows gratitude to become part of our thinking because we allow and accept that all things are good in our lives.

2. *Non-resistance.* Having the mental attitude that what is, just is. When utilizing this principle we gratefully accept and permit what it is that is presenting itself in the moment. We all too often think to ourselves we "should" have done this, or we "should" have done that. By resisting what is we prolong that which we wish to move on from.

3. *Happiness with a state of dissatisfaction.* What we want to strive for is a pure state of happiness. The word happiness relates to joy and gratitude. Yet we also want to grow and

increase our current situation with the ideal that we are always making forward progress on becoming a better person. When we have become satisfied with something we have accepted the status quo, we are stagnant in our upward expansion. "The place you want to be is happy and dissatisfied! In other words, to be thrilled with what you have, joyful and grateful for your accomplishments and blessings, and at the same time, enthusiastic about your ability to do even better."

4. *Forgiveness.* To forgive means to *let go completely* ... This means forgiving other people who you feel have done you wrong as well as forgiving yourself for anything which you have done in the past. The past is finished, we move forward with forgiveness.

   Wes says, "Sorry, but half-baked phony forgiveness won't do the job. You have to do this completely. Forgiveness is not something you do for the other person, it is something you do for yourself."

5. *Give.* We give and then we receive. It is important to give so that we are in flow with the universe, for us to receive what it is that we are asking for. Everything we have been reading about has been in the form of thought; well, giving is our *action.* Keep the flow in your life by being grateful for what is in your life, and then give whatever it is you can.

- Every day just before you go to sleep, list all the things you have to be grateful for.

- Is there anyone you need to forgive who you feel has done you wrong? Put them on your Forgiveness List.

- Have you done something wrong in the past? Put yourself on your Forgiveness List. Is there anything you can do now to right this wrong? Before you *do* anything, call and discuss this with a very trusted advisor. Forgive yourself.

- Give and be open to receiving.

What is at stake?

The man who makes no mistakes
does not usually make anything.

– Edward J. Phelps

"What is at stake if you don't go after your dreams?" I was asked. I felt overcome with emotion as those words went through my mind. A feeling of frustration overwhelmed me.

I thought, "My life would feel empty, I wouldn't feel fulfilled. I would die with the music still in me." This is what I pictured: I'm 90 years old, in my rocking chair, and thinking to myself, "Damn! Why didn't I just go for it?"

"What is it that drives me?" I asked myself.

It is not that I minimized my work, home and family success, but I just felt that I hadn't done anything of significance. It was important to me that I do something significant, something that I found meaningful that would impact helping people. I wanted to make a difference. I couldn't find this in my jobs; I felt empty doing work that didn't give me joy or happiness. I felt unfulfilled.

I knew I wanted more out of life and I believed I deserved it.

The visualization exercise was exactly what I needed to ignite my passion and start pursuing my dream. I decided then that I would no longer be a victim; I needed to stop making excuses and start making decisions. I felt a sense of urgency to my life. I had had a busy career and a busy household, raising two boys, and now that the boys were grown it was time to do what I wanted to do. I no longer wanted to continue to pursue a job for the sake of trading time for money. I believed I had other gifts to share. If I didn't start following my passion now, I thought, then when would be a good time?

Who said that we have to be miserable in a job or doing work we don't enjoy? Yet, so many people continue in a job or stay in work that is empty and without meaning out of fear. Many of us fear what might happen if we take a chance. I suggest you instead look at what you have at stake if you don't change: your life!

I *can't* guarantee you'll live forever if you follow your passion and figure out now how to do what you love. I *can* guarantee, however, that you will live an empty life without happiness if you continue to do something you don't enjoy. Your unhappiness will affect you and everyone around you.

Some people stay in a job just for the money and the benefits and the job title. The money is nice because it allows us to buy stuff. Someone said that "job" stands for "just over broke." People buy things, which put them in debt. They think about getting sick and are glad to have the benefits, and the job title is important to people because it helps them tell us what they do. Their self-identity is wrapped up in their title. The problem with that is people avoid becoming self-aware and knowing who they are. I believe they are afraid to stop and look inside.

Working in a job that does not align with what is most

important to you will leave you empty. What is worse, and we see it often, is people who stay in work they don't enjoy and the job ends up killing them. Literally! How sad is that?! Others wait it out until they retire and find that they have nothing to go to from retirement, and they are very unhappy and bored.

If you wait for permission from someone else to change, in order for you to do the work you love, you may be waiting a long time. You may find, like I did, that you don't have much support for your dreams. It was too "out there" for my family. For them, a job meant security. Again, don't wait for permission.

Some people just wait for retirement. As far as I'm concerned, if you are in a job that you don't enjoy and you are just waiting for retirement, then you are already dead. You are not living! Do what you love *now*! Follow your passion, not your pension. Don't wait! You will find that you will feel and look younger and you will be happy!

I can guarantee you, when you do work you love, you will never have to work another day in your life. Your vocation becomes your vacation! So ask yourself: "Am I doing what I love? Am I living my best life?"

It is easy to watch from the stands, cheering for a winning team, when we could be one of the players. Fear, lack of motivation and anxiousness can suffocate us and put out the fire, stifling our willingness to embrace all of life that is available to us. We watch others and imagine ourselves in the scenes, yet we don't take action.

There is always risk. There are always the jitters and nervous stress that precedes anything unknown. Yet, if you never leave what is secure and explore the unknown, you will never know what you were capable of. It was with determination and repeated attempts after denials and rejections that great novels have been published. It was with many defeated attempts and then more training and hard work that records have been broken.

To just exist in a world where there is great potential would be like dying a slow, agonizing death. You can make a difference. You were born for great things; you have the ability to do anything you want. How would you feel knowing, when your day on this earth has ended, you made a difference? Start today!

Here are some questions to ask yourself in order to go after your dreams.

What Is at Stake? — Notes

1. What is at stake, if I keep doing work that brings no joy or happiness?

2. What is at stake, if I stay in work that is empty and without meaning?

3. What is at stake, if I keep doing work that does not align with my abilities and interests or with what is most important to me?

4. What is at stake, if I keep working for someone else when I would like to start my own business?

5. What is at stake, if I stay in a job *just* for the money?

6. What is at stake, if I don't go for my dream?

Are You Committed?

*We can do anything we want as
long as we stick with it long enough.*

– Helen Keller

Quitting was never an option.

Now, I'm not saying that it was easy to stay committed, and it would have been very easy to quit, but I couldn't look myself in the mirror knowing I had taken the easy way out and just quit.

Whether my studies took years or my workouts took minutes, I didn't even once consider quitting. I was committed to completing anything I started. I read not long ago, "Winners never quit, and quitters never win." I consider myself a winner. That quote has been etched in my head and it motivates me to finish whatever I start. It definitely has kept me motivated to finish my book!

If I say I'm going to do something, I do it. I am committed!

I believe commitment is a key ingredient in success, and staying committed to the end reveals a lot about a person. Committed people don't quit. Thomas Edison tried 1,000 times before his invention of the light bulb came to fruition. Imagine if Thomas Edison was not committed to his invention and he quit trying at the 999th time? Where would we be without electricity?! Aren't you glad he was committed? I sure am!

This is not to say that even being totally committed you won't be faced with challenges or obstacles. Even the best planning cannot predict every obstacle, but when you are committed you will find the ways around problems as they arise.

A good example that most people can relate to is making New Year's resolutions. At one time I looked at a brand new year to set new goals, but as time went on I realized I didn't need to wait for a new year to move forward with my goals. In January the gym is just packed, and after a month and then another month, the attendance dwindles.

Just the other day I ran into a woman I had met at the gym. I hadn't seen her there in quite awhile. I thought she changed the time she worked out and perhaps I just missed her. She told me that she doesn't have the time. People like this are not committed and are always looking for the exit door. This woman wanted to get fit and lose weight. Something motivated her to start going to the gym, but she did not follow through. This woman, like countless others, had lost focus! I couldn't help but think if it was a dentist appointment she would have been there, because more than likely that would be marked down on her planner. It was scheduled in. The same holds true for a workout: schedule it in your day planner and it will get done.

Focus on your commitment!

I had no idea how I was going to fit in full-time studies alongside a full-time job while being a full-time mom, but I made the commitment to change my life, and I knew if I took the action to pursue a degree, I would find my way. I made the promise to myself and resolved that I would do it and I took deliberate action.

There is also something that you need to know about the relationship between goals and commitment. The larger your goal is, the longer it is going to take to reach your outcome and the greater the commitment it will require. The longer it is going to take to achieve the goal, the more time and opportunities there are for things to happen that invite you to veer off course from your goal. This surely happened often while I was pursuing studies in my University degree program. In order to succeed, you must keep your focus on your goal. Certainly there will be distractions, but it is up to you to not lose focus on what you want to accomplish. Stay committed to your success.

When you're committed to your success, your determination will work with your commitment to help keep you moving forward in the face of all the challenges and obstacles that will try to hold you back. Determination and commitment will help you to accept these challenges and look for ways to overcome them. You may tell yourself that you're "committed" to getting a new job … or starting a business … or becoming wealthy … or getting a book published … but have you really committed yourself to doing *all* the little—and big—tasks that are necessary to achieve that goal? Are you committed to making *all* the necessary sacrifices?

That's what commitment to a goal is really about.

So … how do you commit yourself then?

You'll hear people talk about visualization, affirmations, positive self-talk and other techniques designed to "re-program" your mind so that you're compelled to fulfill your commitment. You'll also hear many people claim that these techniques don't work!

Well, it doesn't matter "what works"—what matters is "what works for *you*."

And what works for you is ... *what has worked for you before*!

You see, you've already committed to achieving goals in the past ... and you've achieved those goals. So why not do what you did then in order to commit yourself now?

For example, if you're starting a new hobby, you might recall that when you embraced other hobbies in the past you did specific things that helped you learn a lot about the hobby and develop key skills in a relatively short period of time. It might have been purchasing books and magazines related to the hobby, visiting relevant websites and/or joining groups of like-minded people to discuss and take part in the hobby.

Not only are these activities enjoyable and valuable in themselves, but they also form your commitment ritual, which essentially enables you to fully commit to, and stick with, the new hobby.

Are You Committed? — Notes

Here are five tips to help you stay committed to your goals:

1. Choose a goal that excites you and acknowledge that you are starting a long journey. If you think of it as a sprint, you are more likely to become frustrated.

2. Show your progress to people who will support you in your goal. They will be your cheering squad and you will be encouraged to continue pursuing your goal until you reach it.

3. Give yourself short-term goals (i.e., bench press 40 pounds by the end of the first month of weight training).

These short-term goals will inspire you to set more short-term goals.

4. Look back at how far you've come—celebrate your progress.

5. Keep on keeping on! You can do it!

10

Getting Started

A s you can see, I am just an ordinary woman, who had ordinary challenges; I overcame them, because I was persistent and I was determined to achieve success—no matter what! I hope my story has helped you to reflect on your life, and I'm hopeful that you will see the lessons in all your experiences. I hope I have inspired you to embrace your challenges, face your fears, take risks and grow. Go for your dreams! You can do it!

As Denis Waitley put it:

> *Get excited and enthusiastic about your own dreams.*
> *This excitement is like a forest fire—you can smell it, taste*
> *it, and see it from a mile away!*

My purpose in writing my book was to share my experiences, so that it would encourage, motivate, inspire and empower other women and men to go for their dreams.

If I have accomplished this, then you are probably either very scared or very excited; these are the two emotions you will experience when you know you are ready to move forward.

If you are truly serious about change, you need to take action … *now*! If you don't, this book, with all its information, and potential for getting you and your dreams together, is of no value. Knowledge is powerful only when applied.

How you can get started …

If you haven't already done so, take some time right away to complete the suggestions that are at the end of each section in all of the chapters.

Below, I've given you a "short list" to complete. It works best if you write out your thoughts. By doing this, it will help you focus on what you want and give clarity about what you don't want. As someone once said: "Writing is the doing part of thinking."

1. Imagine your life ending. Will you have regrets about the things you didn't do?

2. Think about how you feel about yourself. Do you have a healthy self-image? If you don't, are you ready and willing to change that?

3. What choices have you made that are not serving you anymore? (HINT: Your job? Ignoring your dreams?) Make a list.

4. What choice or choices can you make *today* to start the changes you want? (HINT: Instead of watching TV for 30 minutes, how about going for a walk for 30 minutes. Another hint: Need to return some phone calls? How about setting a timer—start at the sound of the bell. One more hint: Do you really have to read *every* e-mail? Delete or unsubscribe to those e-mails.)

5. What area in your life is causing you the *most* pain? Is this more painful than the pain of changing?

6. Think of a time when you experienced an accident, loss, tragedy or any other unwelcome event. How did you respond? Did you or could have you turned that event into something good?

7. What is your greatest fear?

8. What is the one thing that you would do if you knew you could not fail?

9. List all the skills you developed. How have they helped shape your life?

NEXT ...

Write out your *biggest* wishes and dreams. Let's consider these your goals!

AND THEN ...

Within the next 24 hours, identify one small step you can do that will help you move toward your goal. This exercise can be done daily and you can use it as a way to measure your progress and keep you moving toward your goal. A good idea would be to purchase a journal so you can keep all the entries in one location.

Now remember, it is imperative that you take action immediately, within the next 24 hours, because you are excited about going after your dreams. By taking action, you will gain momentum and, like an airplane about to take off the runway, you will be airborne before you know it.

Each day, complete this sentence: "Within the next 24 hours I will _____ ."

THEN NEXT ...
To greatly enhance your ability to accomplish your goals and dreams, you must get a coach. Use the questions I've outlined to assist you in identifying a great coach.

FINALLY ...
Throughout my book, I've highlighted a number of characteristics that were paramount in my success and you can develop them. You will find that once you have developed these, you are ready to be the person you want to become and you will become unstoppable.

+ Be persistent
+ Stay motivated
+ Keep inspired
+ Stay determined
+ Stay committed
+ Watch your words
+ Keep a positive attitude
+ Picture or imagine your dream
+ Believe you will succeed
+ Develop good habits
+ Manage your time
+ Expect roadblocks
+ Always be grateful

- Expect success
- Never give up
- Be unstoppable

EXPECT SUCCESS —
BE UNSTOPPABLE!

If you are reading this, there is no doubt that either you have been inspired to go after your dreams and/or you somehow abandoned your dreams, but *now* they have been reignited. I encourage you to keep your dreams alive. Here is how you can get started; I'm inviting you to go here for a:

Complimentary Strategy Coaching Session

Contact your Unstoppable Success Coach, Julie,
e-mail Julie@expectsuccessbeunstoppable.com
or call 701-205-4077

References and Quotation Sources

Abraham-Hicks, Abraham-Hicks Publications
  ✦ www.abraham-hicks.com

Aldana, Jacquelyn (*The 15-Minute Miracle Revealed*™)

Alexander, Lloyd (1974–2007)

Allenbaugh Ph.D., Eric Allenbaugh & Assoc.
  ✦ www.allenbaugh.com

Angelou, Maya ✦ www.mayaangelou.com

Bristol, Claude M. ✦ www.laudebristol.wwwhubs.com

Brooke, Richard B. ✦ www.selfgrowth.com

Brown, Jr., H. Jackson ✦ www.instructionbook.com

Brown, Les ✦ www.lesbrown.com

Butterworth, Eric ✦ www.ericbutterworth.org

Byrd, Michael K.

Cameron, Julia ✦ www.theartistsway.com/about/julia-cameron

Canfield, Jack ✦ www.jackcanfield.com

Cathcart, Jim ✦ www.cathcart.com

Chopra, Deepak ✦ www.chopra.com

Conklin, Robert ✦ www.facebook.com/people/Robert-Conklin

Coolidge, Calvin (1872–1933)

Covey, Stephen R. ✦ www.stephencovey.com

DeVos, Richard M., Founder of Amway

Di Lemme, John ✦ www.FindYourWhy.com

Disraeli, Benjamin (1804–1881)

Dunnington, Lewis L. (1867–1936)

Dyer, Dr. Wayne W. ✦ www.drwaynedyer.com

Evans, Marsha ✦ www.forbes.com/marchajevans

Ewing, Sam (1920–2001) ✦ www.basicfamouspeople.com

Ford, Henry ✦ www.hfmgv.org/EXHIBITS/HF

Goethe, Johann Wolfgang von (1774–1832) author, poet

Gorman, Mark ✦ www.markgorman.com

Halsey, Jr., William F. "Bull" (1882–1959) ✦ www.history.navy.mil

Hanh Thich Nhat ✦ www.plumvillage.org

Hill, Napoleon ✦ www.naphill.org

James, William ✦ www.des.emory.edu/mfp/jphotos

Jesse, Owens ✦ www.jesseewilliams.org

Jimenez, M.Ed., Lisa ✦ www.RX-Success.com

Jones, Charles "Tremendous" ✦ www.executivebooks.com/cjones

Jordan, Michael ✦ www.23jordan.com

Keller, Helen (1880–1968) ✦ www.afb.org/braillebug/helenkeller

King Jr., Dr. Martin Luther (1929–1968)
    ✦ www.nobelprize.org/king-bio

Korda, Michael ✦ www.phoenix5.org/books/korda

Lakein, Alan ✦ www.linkedin.com/pub/alanlakein

Litman, Mike (audio "Your Greatness Held Hostage")

Lunden, Joan ✦ www.joanlunden.com

Mandela, Nelson ✦ www.anc.org.za/people/mandela

Mandino Og (1923–1996) ✦ www.ogmandino.com

Marden, Orison Swett (1850–1924)
✦ www.infusebooks.com/marden

Marston, Jr., Ralph S. ✦ www.greatday.com

Nichols, Lisa (audio) ✦ www.lisa-nichols.com

Nightingale, Earl, (1921–1989) ✦ www.earlnightingale.com

OPRAH—Winfrey, Oprah ✦ www.oprah.com

Osteen, Joel ✦ www.joelosteen.com

Outlaw, Frank, Founder, Bi-Lo Supermarkets

Perot, H. Ross ✦ www.geocities.com

Phelps, Edward J. (1822–1900) ✦ www.infoplease.com

Proctor, Bob ✦ www.bobproctor.com

Rohn, Jim (audio) ✦ www.jimrohn.com

Roosevelt, Eleanor (1884–1962) ✦ www.fdrlibrary.marist.edu

Ruiz, Don Miguel ✦ www.miguelruiz.com

Schuller, Robert H. ✦ www.crystalcathedral.org,
www.positiveminute@hourofpower.com

Shaw, Henry Wheeler "Josh Billings" (1818–1885)
✦ www.biographybase.com

Shinn, Florence Scovel (1871–1940)
✦ www.florencescovelshinn.wwwhubs.com

Stone, W. Clement (1902–2002)
✦ www.cornerstone.wwwhubs.com/Clement

Stowe, Harriet Beecher (1811–1896) ✦ www.lkwdpl.org

Swindoll, Charles ✦ www.insight.org

Tracy, Brian ✦ www.BrianTracy.com

Twain, Mark (1835–1910) ✦ www.cmgww.com/historic/twain

Waitley, Denis ✦ www.mindperk.com

Wattles, Wallace D. (1860–1911)
   ✦ www.wallacewattles.www.hubs.com

Williamson, Marianne ✦ www.maryannewilliamson.com

ABOUT THE AUTHOR

Julie Henderson is the founder and owner of her own company: EXPECT SUCCESS—BE UNSTOPPABLE. She is a certified coach, entrepreneur, author and speaker. She began this company to be able to provide strategies for anyone who has a desire to better their life.

Her passion is to motivate, inspire, encourage and empower others to create an exciting future for themselves, and not to give up on their dreams—*ever*!

Julie has over 20 years of success helping people achieve their dreams and the life they want for themselves—despite *any* obstacles.

Read about Julie's life-changing event! She understands life challenges and how difficult these can be, especially when no one really understands what you are going through.

Julie grew up on a small family farm in Saskatchewan, Canada. She is the second child of six, with a brother and four sisters. The whole family worked on the farm.

As she grew up, Julie dreamed big dreams for her life. From this modest beginning, and despite many setbacks, discouragements and lack of support from family who did not really understand her dream, Julie set out to manifest her vision.

She is a University graduate from Alberta, Canada, and a Registered Nutritional Consultant. She holds a certification through Professional Secretaries International, as well as Fitness and Customer Service Trainer. Her experience includes Senior Executive, Instructor, Training Consultant and Manager of Student Services. She was a member of Toastmasters International. She is the author of numerous articles, reports and her blog *Women's Success Secrets* at www.expectsuccessbeunstoppable.com/blog.

Julie is your Unstoppable Success Coach!